true alchemy
or the quest
for perfection

Cover illustration: a crystal

Omraam Mikhaël Aïvanhov

true alchemy or the quest for perfection

Translated from the French
2nd edition

Collection Izvor
No. 221

EDITIONS PROSVETA

By the same author :
(translated from the French)

Izvor Collection

201 — Toward a Solar Civilization
202 — Man, Master of his Destiny
203 — Education Begins Before Birth
204 — The Yoga of Nutrition
205 — Sexual Force or the Winged Dragon
206 — A Philosophy of Universality
207 — What is a Spiritual Master ?
208 — The Egregor of the Dove or the Reign of Peace
209 — Christmas and Easter in the Initiatic Tradition
210 — The Tree of the Knowledge of Good and Evil
211 — Freedom, the Spirit Triumphant
212 — Light is a Living Spirit
213 — Man's Two Natures : Human and Divine
214 — Hope for the World : Spiritual Galvanoplasty
215 — The True Meaning of Christ's Teaching
216 — The Living Book of Nature
217 — New Light on the Gospels
218 — The Symbolic Language of Geometrical Figures
219 — Man's Subtle Bodies and Centres
220 — The Zodiac, Key to Man and to the Universe
221 — True Alchemy or the Quest for Perfection
222 — Man's Psychic Life : Elements and Structures
223 — Creation : Artistic and Spiritual

Forthcoming
224 — The Powers of Thought

Prosveta S.A. — B.P. 12 — 83601 Fréjus Cedex (France)

ISBN 2-85566-384-9
édition originale : 2-85566-348-2

TABLE OF CONTENTS

One   Spiritual Alchemy 9

Two   The Human Tree 21

Three   Character and Temperament 33

Four   Our Heritage from the Animal
           Kingdom 45

Five   Fear 59

Six   Stereotypes 73

Seven   Grafting 89

Eight   The Use of Energy 101

Nine   Sacrifice, the Transmutation
           of Matter 113

Ten   Vainglory and Divine Glory 135

Eleven   Pride and Humility 153

Twelve   The Sublimation of Sexual Energy . 173

The reader will better understand certain aspects of the lectures published in the present volume if he bears in mind that the Master Omraam Mikhaël Aïvanhov's Teaching is exclusively oral.

1

SPIRITUAL ALCHEMY

It often happens that somebody comes to consult me about a problem: he tells me that he has a terrible vice and the poor fellow is miserable and completely discouraged because, although he has been trying for years to overcome it, it always gets the better of him. When I hear him explaining all this I exclaim, 'Oh, but that's magnificent! Wonderful! That just proves that you are very, very strong!' He looks at me in astonishment and begins to wonder if I'm not laughing at him. 'No, no,' I assure him; 'I'm not laughing at you. It's just that you don't recognize your own strength.' 'What strength? I always give in. The temptation always gets the better of me. Doesn't that show how weak I am!' But I tell him, 'No, I can't accept that; your reasoning is at fault. If I explain exactly how it all happened you will realize that I'm not joking.

'Who formed that vice in the first place?' I ask him. 'Wasn't it you? To begin with it was no bigger than a snowball in your hand, but as you went on adding to it and amusing yourself by rolling it in the snow, it got bigger and bigger until it became a mountain, and now it is blocking your path. To begin with, the vice you are so upset about was no more than a tiny thought in your mind, but you harboured and nourished it, in other words, you "rolled it in the snow" and now you're overwhelmed by it. But what is striking in this is your strength! After all, it was you who made this vice what it is today. It was you who fathered it, and now it is your son and he's so big and strong that you can't get the better of him. You should be very proud!' 'Proud! How can I be proud of that?' he objects. 'Haven't you read Gogol's short story about Taras Bulba?' I ask him. 'No? Well then I'll tell you about it. It is very instructive!'

'Taras Bulba was an old Cossack who had sent his two sons to college in Kiev. When they went home after three years at college, Taras Bulba was delighted to see that they had turned out to be two stalwart young men. In his pride and joy and as a sign of his fatherly affection (Cossacks sometimes have strange ways of expressing their affection, you know!) he began to pummel them with his fists. But the boys had no intention of letting themselves be punched, even by their father, so they punched back and soon knocked him down. Perhaps you think that, as he scrambled to his feet a little the worse for wear, Taras Bulba was furious, but not at all: he was as proud as he could be at having fathered two such vigorous young men!

'So why not be like Taras Bulba and take pride in your son who has become so much stronger than his father? You are the father. It was you who made him strong by feeding him with your thoughts and desires, so you must be very strong yourself. And now I'll tell you how you can beat him. What does a man do when he wants to bring a wild, extravagant son to his senses? He cuts off his allowance, of course, and having no more money, the boy is forced to reason and change his ways. So why keep your son supplied with food and money? Do you want him to go on defying you? Why not cut off his allowance? Since it was you who brought him into existence you have authority over him, but if you don't exercise your authority you'll spend the rest of your life struggling and suffering without ever finding the way out of your difficulties.'

Unfortunately there are not many people who manage to look at things this way. They struggle desperately against their own pernicious tendencies, without at all realizing that if they are in such dire straits today it is because they are extraordinarily strong. The stronger the enemy within, the more it shows how strong you yourself are. Yes, this is how you should look at the situation.

Have you never observed how tense you get when you're struggling against yourself, and how difficult so many things seem to be? A terrible battle rages within you and plunges you into all kinds of conflicting situations. You have the impression that the whole of your lower nature is necessarily an enemy and you want to kill it. But that enemy is very powerful: the war you have been waging against it for centuries has only strengthened it; it becomes more of a threat every day. It is true, of course, that we do have enemies within us, but if they are our enemies it is mainly because we are very poor alchemists and are incapable of performing the necessary transformations.

Do you remember what St. Paul said? 'A thorn in the flesh was given to me... I pleaded with the Lord three times that it might depart from me. And he said to me, "My grace is sufficient for you, for My strength is made perfect in weakness": Someone who has a weakness of body, heart or mind feels that it lessens his worth, but in this he is mistaken: that weakness can be a valuable source of enrichment. If all his aspirations

were already fulfilled he would be in danger of
stagnating. If he wants to advance he needs something to spur him on, and it is this weakness, this
'thorn in the flesh' which forces him to work hard
to transform himself in depth, to draw ever closer
to Heaven and to the Lord. The Lord leaves us
with certain weaknesses in order to incite us to
greater efforts in our spiritual work : that which
seems to us to be a weakness may, in fact, be a
strength.

Weaknesses must be put to work : they have
to make themselves useful. Probably you are puz-
zled when I say that ; you had always thought that
they had to be trampled underfoot and extermi-
nated. Well, just try it and you'll soon see that it is
not easy : you are the one who is likely to be trampled underfoot! The problem is the same for
every form of vice and every failing, whether it be
greed, sensuality, violence, covetousness or
vanity : you have to know how to enrol their energies in the service of your own cause, how to get
them to work with you towards your chosen goal.
If you work alone you will never succeed. If you
banish all your enemies, everything that stands
up to you, who is going to work for you? Who
will serve you?

By dint of great patience men have tamed
and domesticated several different kinds of wild
animals which are now very useful to them.

Horses used to be wild and dogs were as savage as wolves, and if man was able to domesticate them it was because he had developed certain qualities in himself. He is certainly capable of taming and domesticating other wild beasts, but in order to do so he needs to develop other qualities.

So be glad : you are all very wealthy since you all have weaknesses ! But it is essential that you learn how to handle them and put them to work. I took the example of animals, just now, but you could take the example of natural forces such as lightning, electricity, fire and flood. Now that man knows how to control them he uses them for his own enrichment and yet, before he learned to control them, they were hostile to him. People find it normal to use the forces of nature, but if one suggests that they might learn to use the gales, storms, waterfalls and thunderbolts that rage within them they are very astonished. And yet nothing is more natural, and once you know the rules of spiritual alchemy you will learn how to transform and use even the poisons in you. Yes, for hatred, anger, jealousy and so on are poisons, but in the Universal White Brotherhood you learn how to use these poisons. In fact you will be given the methods you need to make use of all the negative forces which are so plentiful within you. So, be glad, for there is a bright future ahead of you !

In the future, those who have the courage to do so will study these dangerous chemical substances: jealousy, hatred, fear, sexual energy, etc., and learn to use them. In fact they will bottle them and keep them in their medicine cupboards so as to have them to hand whenever they need them. As you can see, all the preconceived notions in your heads are going to have to change from now on!

Now, of course, you must not throw yourself full tilt into evil and try to swallow great chunks of it. In every human being, even the best, there are always some diabolical tendencies, survivors from a far-distant past, and you have to be very careful not to let them loose all at once, on the pretext that you want to use them. You have to probe the depths gently and bring up only a few atoms, a few electrons, and be sure to digest them thoroughly. It is not a question of launching recklessly into combat against infernal forces, for they would simply destroy you. You have to know how to set about it. This is why you must continue to work with the forces from on high, using the weapons of prayer, harmony and love and, from time to time, when some creature emerges from your inner depths and attacks you with tooth and nail and claw in an effort to get you to do something really stupid, catch it, study it closely in your laboratory and force it to give up its venom

so that you can use it. If you do this you will find
that evil can give you just that element you
needed for fulfilment.

But, I repeat, be careful! Don't use what I
have just told you to go rushing off to confront
evil in its lair. Don't think, 'Aha, now I understand! Well, you just watch and you'll see what I
can do!' because it is quite possible that, on the
contrary, you will never be seen again! It has
already happened to some who thought they were
very strong but who had neglected to build a
strong alliance with good and light, and now the
poor creatures are in a pitiful state. All their negative forces have pounced on them to plunder and
despoil them.

The Talmud says that, in the last days, the
Righteous, that is to say, Initiates, will eat the
flesh of the Leviathan, the monster that lives at
the bottom of the sea. Yes, the Leviathan is going
to be caught and cut up and salted — and kept in
our freezers I suppose! Then, when the time is
ripe, the Righteous will gather to feast off its
flesh. What a delightful thought! If we had to
take that literally I'm sure that many fastidious,
Christian people would be thoroughly disgusted.
So we must interpret it to see what it means: the
Leviathan is a collective being which represents
all the entities of the astral plane (symbolized by
the ocean), and it is destined to become a festive

dish for the Righteous, which means that he who is capable of dominating and using the lusts and passions of his astral dimension will find in them a rich source of benefits and blessings.

2

THE HUMAN TREE

We all possess certain organs whose functions seem to us neither very spiritual nor very beautiful — nor even very clean — but which are, nevertheless, very necessary, for every cell and every organ in our body is linked to other organs and cells, just as the roots of a tree are linked to the branches, leaves, flowers and fruit. If a man cuts off his roots, that is to say if he eliminates the organs which constitute the foundation of his existence he will suffer terrible consequences. True, these organs are sometimes the cause of tragedies, but even so he must allow them to go on living and try to transform them and draw strength from them.

If you read the biographies of famous people you will often be astonished to see how many of them had abnormal and even monstrous criminal tendencies in their make-up. If you don't understand the pattern on which man is built, this may seem to be an unacceptable contradiction. How is it possible? In point of fact the explanation is very simple: these men and women were constantly obliged to resist and struggle against their criminal tendencies and thanks to this struggle they managed, whether they fully realized it or not, to graft good onto the evil which lurked in the depths of their being. The more daunting, the more ardent their passions (their roots), the sweeter and more delectable their fruits, the more remarkable their achievements. Whereas so many others, who had none of these hideous defects, remained sterile, leading mediocre, insignificant lives and contributing nothing to the common good of mankind.

Now, I don't mean to say that we should excuse, still less cultivate, our evil tendencies. Certainly not! But we must try to understand this sublime philosophy which teaches how to use the forces of evil in order to create something truly splendid. The higher the trunk and branches of a tree reach in their upward thrust, the deeper are the roots it plunges into the soil. Anyone who has not grasped this is appalled by the all-pervasiveness of evil. But you must not be afraid: everything in nature is designed in accordance with marvellously wise laws. If our roots do not reach deep enough we shall be unable to draw the nutritional elements we need from the earth or to stand up to the storms of life.

Now, let's look closer at this analogy between man and a tree. The roots of the tree correspond to a man's stomach and sexual organs. Yes, man is rooted in the earth by means of his stomach which enables him to nourish himself, and by his sexual organs which enable him to reproduce. The trunk of the tree is represented in man by the lungs and heart, that is to say, by the respiratory and circulatory systems, with their arterial and venous circuits. The downward circuit flows from the leaves, carrying the sugar sap with which it nourishes the whole tree, while the upward circuit carries the raw mineral juices up

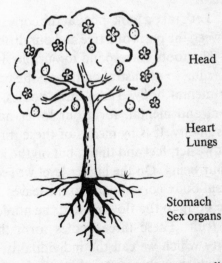

Head

Heart
Lungs

Stomach
Sex organs

Figure 1 — The parts of a tree and the corresponding human organs

into the leaves to be converted into sap. In our bodies we can see the same principle at work in the circulation of the blood: the arterial circuit transports the clean, pure blood throughout the body while the venous circuit carries the impure blood back to the lungs. The two currents work together for the health and well-being of the human tree.

The leaves, flowers and fruit of a tree correspond to our head. A man's fruits are his thoughts: it is in his head, in his mind, that a man is fruitful. But the roots, the trunk, branches and leaves, the flowers and fruit are all interconnected.

Let's take a look, now, at the correspondence between the parts of a tree and our different bodies. The roots correspond to our physical body; the trunk to our astral body, and the branches to our mental body. These three bodies, physical, astral and mental, form our lower nature, our personality. It is by means of these three bodies that we act, feel and think, but on the lower level of our being. On the higher level we see that the causal body corresponds to the leaves; the buddhic body to the flowers, and the atmic body to the fruit. These three bodies form the higher trinity which we call the individuality, and it is they which enable man to think, feel and act in the higher planes.

HIGHER NATURE

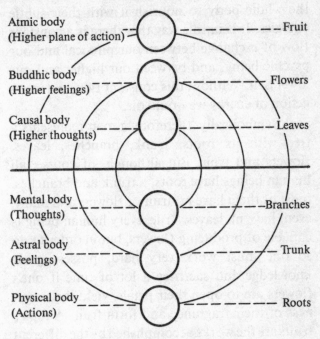

Atmic body
(Higher plane of action) ———— Fruit

Buddhic body
(Higher feelings) ———— Flowers

Causal body
(Higher thoughts) ———— Leaves

Mental body
(Thoughts) ———— Branches

Astral body
(Feelings) ———— Trunk

Physical body
(Actions) ———— Roots

LOWER NATURE

Figure 2 — Correspondences between the parts of a tree and
man's six bodies

The stomach, for example, is a factory which
transforms raw materials: here lie the roots of
our physical being. The raw materials which have
been fed to the stomach to be transformed, are
then further processed by the lungs, heart and
brain, becoming thoughts and feelings, and these

thoughts and feelings are, in turn, sent down into the whole body to nourish it with their subtle energies. It is in this way that there is a constant flow of exchange between our physical and our psychic being, and between our higher and our lower Self. Without this constant flow and inter-action of energy we would die.

Symbolically, therefore, a man represents a tree with its roots, trunk, branches, leaves, flowers and fruit. But although, of course, all human beings have roots, a trunk and branches, most of them have no fruit or flowers and many, even, have no leaves. True, every human being is capable of producing flowers, but in order to do so one must work very hard, possess great knowledge and sacrifice a lot of time if one's flowers are to open their petals, yield the sweet-ness of their fragrance and form fruit. A man's fruits are the works accomplished by the different virtues.

Leaves, flowers and fruit represent love, wis-dom and truth. Leaves represent wisdom, flowers love, and fruit truth. But he whose consciousness is bogged down in the lower levels of matter pos-sesses neither light nor warmth nor life; he lives only on the grosser, denser level of the three lower bodies, physical, astral and mental. Movement, warmth and light are manifested only in the leaves, flowers and fruit and he who seeks wisdom, love and truth lives on this level, the level of the three higher bodies.

The roots, therefore, prepare nourishment for the fruit which is ripening on the highest level of one's being. The roots are inseparably connected to the fruit, they are the starting point, while the fruit is the goal or finishing point. Once the fruit has ripened the roots interrupt their activity. The fruits, with the seeds they contain,

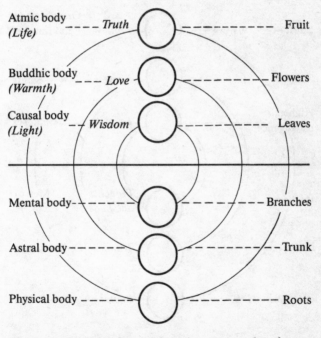

Figure 3 – Wisdom, love and truth correspond to leaves, flowers and fruit

are the roots of the future from which a new stem
will spring. The fact that there are plants which
bear their fruit directly on their roots (tubers) is
an indication of that close relationship between
roots and fruit. Tubers are plants which have
failed to develop on the plane of the spirit: they
have stayed underground.

You can see, too, that there is a link between
the trunk and the flowers as well as between the

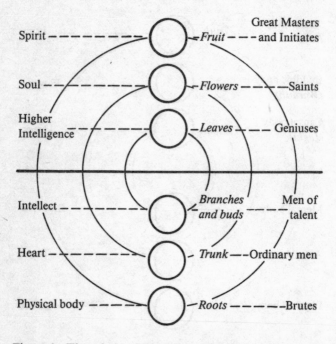

Figure 4 – The relationships between different categories of
human beings

branches and the leaves. Similarly in man, the physical body is linked to the spirit, the heart is linked to the soul and the lower mental body is linked to the higher mental, or Causal, body. This explains why there is a special relationship between Masters and the coarsest, most brutish human beings; between ordinary, common men and saints, and between men of talent and geniuses.

And now let's see what we can learn from the leaves of a tree: leaves transform the raw mineral juices into nutritive sap, just as alchemists transformed base metals into gold with the help of the Philosopher's Stone. Alchemists sought the Philosopher's Stone in order to turn all other metals into gold. True! But an alchemist has to be far more than a good chemist. Nobody expects a chemist to introduce anything other than purely material elements into his experiments, whereas an alchemist has to do so. And this explains why so many alchemists in the past who knew the formula for obtaining the Philosopher's Stone perfectly, never managed to get the desired results in spite of having made all the necessary preparations with the utmost care. They were not true, good alchemists. The true alchemist knows that, in addition to the chemical elements he has to prepare according to the formula, he must also be capable of emanating a force which, alone, can trigger the process of transmutation. A great many men know secret formulas intellectually, in their minds, but they fail to carry their experiments through to the desired conclusion because they do not possess the necessary powers or virtues. Producing the Philosopher's Stone, therefore, is less a physical than a psychic and spiritual process. Someone who wants to obtain the Philosopher's Stone has to begin by studying the virtues and developing them in himself. Only if he does this can he hope to be obeyed by matter.

3

CHARACTER AND TEMPERAMENT

It is commonly said that every living creature, every animal, insect or human being has its own particular character or, to put it in more general terms, its particular characteristics. Also, in everyday conversation, people often confuse the terms 'character' and 'temperament' although, in fact, they are not at all the same thing.

Basically, temperament is something which is related to the vital dimension of man. It is a synthesis of all the instincts, tendencies and impulses which man is virtually incapable of changing or eliminating because they are rooted in his biological and physiological dimension. Temperament, therefore, is closely related to man's animal nature.

Character, on the other hand, while it cannot be dissociated from temperament, represents the intellectual, conscious, voluntary dimension of man. A man's character is the result of his con-

scious effort to modify — by addition or subtrac-
tion — certain aspects of his innate temperament
by the use of his intellectual and emotional faculties and the use of his willpower. Character is the
behaviour of a conscious human being who
knows what he is doing and where he is going,
whereas temperament represents the impulses of
his biological nature, the tendencies which lie
beneath the surface of his consciousness. Character is, as it were, a synthesis of all the particular
characteristics of a man's temperament which
have been conquered and brought under control.

As I have said, it is well-nigh impossible to
change one's temperament, for every human
being born into the world has received a temperament which has been clearly defined in advance.
But as the character is formed by the conscious
tendencies of a being who reasons and reflects
and who wants to assert himself by improving —
or by deteriorating — the heritage he was born
with, this results in an attitude, a way of manifesting oneself which is often in direct contradiction
to one's basic temperament. This is what we mean
by character. A person's character is, as it were, a
new 'version' of his temperament, a version
which has been coloured, modified and oriented
towards a specific goal, an ideal. It is like a
deliberately acquired habit and it becomes
second nature. Character is not something which

exists at birth, it is formed gradually, over the years. You can see this in children: they have a temperament but not yet a character.

Hippocrates distinguished four types or categories of temperament, which he named sanguine, choleric (or bilious), melancholic and phlegmatic, but other classifications exist. In traditional astrology, for instance, there are seven types: Solar, Lunar, Mercurian, Venusian, Martian, Jupiterian and Saturnian. Yet another system distinguishes only three types: Instinctive (those in which the biological dimension is dominant), Sentimental (includes those in which the emotional dimension predominates) and Intellectual (those in which the mental attributes predominate).

So temperament is fixed and unchanging, but a person's environment, family, society, education and so on, all influence his basic temperament and, in so doing, form the character. A person's character is formed under the influence of his environment and the conditions in which he lives, and this is why it can either improve or deteriorate. His conscious, individual will is an important factor in the formation of character for it reveals what he has decided or accepted to be, but the influence of others is also very important.

There is no need for me to explain, yet again, that if we are born with a certain type of temperament it is for a good reason. As you know, it is a consequence of former lives, former incarnations: in the past, each person has allied himself, by means of his thoughts, desires and actions, with certain forces which now determine his subconscious, that is to say his temperament, and there is not much he can do about it. Temperament is like the skeleton: it cannot be radically changed. You cannot enlarge your skull, lengthen your nose or remodel a receding chin. Similarly, although everything in nature can be transformed by the power of thought and will, nevertheless, any changes effected in the unconscious elements which constitute the temperament are so slow and so imperceptible that one can almost say that they don't happen in this incarnation. Character, on the other hand, can be changed, modelled and improved; in fact this is the principal task of a disciple of a spiritual Teaching.

Take the case of someone who is very dynamic and hotheaded and even violent. He is so curt and dogmatic that he can hardly open his mouth without wounding other people's feelings or trampling on their interests. His impulsive temperament is the cause of frequent explosions and eruptions! But then, one day, realizing that his attitude is extremely detrimental to himself he takes himself in hand and, after a while, by dint of willpower, he manages to soften his character and stop riding roughshod over everybody. He is still quite capable of reacting violently — this will be true to the end of his days — but thanks to his strong will he has learned to control himself and find just the right word, the appropriate expression or gesture that offends no one. This is character.

Character, therefore, is a pattern of behaviour (both in regard to oneself and in regard to others) which has been grafted onto the basic temperament. It is an attitude, a way of behaving, which results from the union and integration of various elements, strengths or weaknesses.

A disciple's work must be based on an understanding of this question of temperament and character so that, even if he is not pre-disposed by his temperament, he can still forge a character of exceptional goodness, magnanimity and generosity. It is not easy, I grant you that: if it were, everybody would already have a perfectly divine character, but at least one can and must work towards it.

Take the example of a tree: where is the temperament of a tree? In its roots. It is the roots which determine the shape and size and strength and all the particular qualities of a tree. As for its

character, well, of course, a tree cannot really
have a character, but still, its fruit and flowers
have their own special properties (astringent, lax-
ative, soothing, stimulating, nourishing, etc.,
etc.): you could say that they represent the
'character' of the tree. But a tree could never
produce these characteristic manifestations, it
could never produce flowers or fruit if it had no
roots. And similarly, man could not have a
character if he had no temperament. His temperament is the storehouse from which he draws the
elements used in forming his character. It is like a
factory or a laboratory: the particular articles or
products manufactured are determined by the
type of chemicals or raw materials and machines
available.

Animals cannot be said to have character.
The character of cats, dogs or mice is simply their
particular way of biting, scratching, barking, eating or running, etc. It does not amount to very
much. Animals have only their temperament for,
as I have just explained, character is something
which man himself fashions consciously, and
animals have no way of improving or changing
themselves: they are as nature has made them.
The difference, therefore, between men and
animals, is that animals are bound by their temperament, they are condemned to remain within
the limits imposed by nature, they are faithful to

their instinct. When animals attack and devour each other there is no blame attached, they are innocent because they are not breaking the laws of nature. On the contrary, their behaviour is in keeping with those laws. Whereas men have all kinds of possibilities and very favourable conditions in order to transform themselves for better or for worse, and they also have the possibility of breaking the natural law and refusing to obey.

And now we come to a very practical question: how to transform oneself. Of course, this is a very difficult task; the matter of which our physical and psychic being is composed is tough and unyielding and it cannot easily be shaped and remodelled. However, it can be done if one knows how, and we shall now see how.

Matter exists in four different forms, solid, liquid, gaseous and igneous, which correspond to the four elements, earth, water, air and fire. On an ascending scale, each element is subtler and less stable than those below it. These four major categories of matter can also be seen in man: his physical body corresponds to earth; his astral body (heart) corresponds to water; his mental body (intellect) corresponds to air, and his causal body (spirit) corresponds to fire. And now, in order to understand the relations that exist between the different elements, we have to read a page from the great book of living Nature.

One day I met someone who was just coming back from a stroll by the sea. I asked him, 'What did you see, there?' 'Oh, nothing much.' 'What? You didn't notice anything?' I asked. 'No, there was nothing special to see. The sea was calm and the sun was shining. That's all.' 'Ah, but there was something absolutely vital to see, something that could have transformed you and changed your whole life if you had seen and understood it!' Of course, he looked at me in utter bewilderment, so I said, 'Did you see the rocks?' 'Yes.' 'And did you notice how intricately they are shaped?' 'Yes.' 'Who sculptured them, do you suppose?' 'Why, the water, of course; the pounding of the waves.' 'Yes, and who moved the water?' 'The air.' 'Yes, and who caused the air to move?' 'Well, I suppose it must be the sun.' 'Exactly! There we have it!' But he was still staring at me and had not understood what I was getting at. I will explain.

The sun causes the air to move; the air acts upon the water and the water acts on the earth. Let me interpret that: the spirit acts upon the mind, the mind acts upon the heart and the heart acts upon the physical body. That is why you have to learn to work with your spirit, for it is the spirit that will illuminate the mind; the mind, in turn, will enlighten the heart, and the heart will purify the physical body. Yes, if you understand how the four elements work together you will be capable of transforming yourself by forging your own character and, eventually, even your temperament may be affected. It is possible, therefore, to transform oneself completely, but on condition that one begins at the beginning: with the spirit. Establish a sublime being, a high ideal, firmly in your spirit and concentrate on it every single day: the new vibrations it brings with it will amplify and spread out within you and penetrate to the depths of your being.

Needless to say, this is a task that is going to take a long time before you see any results, but you must not let that discourage you. Look how long it has taken for the sea to shape the rocks along the shore! So take heart and persevere, and one day you will find that you have fashioned your own 'rocks', your own physical body.

4

OUR HERITAGE FROM
THE ANIMAL KINGDOM

A human being is a synthesis of all that exists in the universe. This being so you need not be astonished if I say that all the animals that have ever existed are present in man's make-up, they dwell in his subconscious in the form of instincts, impulses and tendencies. Our instincts and passions represent a whole host of animals for which we are responsible: we have to tame them and put them to work exactly as, in the past, men tamed horses, oxen, dogs, goats, cats, sheep, camels, elephants, etc., and used them to help him in his labours.

When Adam and Eve lived in the Garden of Eden they had a brotherly relationship with all the animals, and the animals themselves lived in perfect peace with each other. It was Adam who looked after them and they all understood and obeyed him. Perhaps you will object that you have never read about that in any history books. I

know. But if you had access to the Akashic
Records, the annals of humanity, you would find
out that before the Fall, when human beings were
still full of light, knowledge, beauty and power,
all the forces of nature were in harmony with
them and obeyed them. Then, later, when man
chose to listen to other voices and follow the bid-
ding of another, symbolized in Genesis by the
Serpent, his inner light abandoned him and, at
the same time, he lost his power over the animals,
and the animals were divided amongst themselves: some remained faithful to man whilst
others declared war on him, for they could not
forgive him for his fault.

I know, of course, that most people are unable to accept such an idea; they can see no relationship at all between their own nature and that
of the animals. But I can assure you that many of
our inner states of mind are in the form of tigers,
wild boars, crocodiles, leopards, cobras, scor-
pions and octopuses, whereas others take the
shape of gentle, lovable little birds. Swarms of
wild animals live inside each one of us. If you are
under the impression that all those prehistoric
animals — dinosaurs, diplodocuses, ichthyosauri
and pterosaurs — have all disappeared, then you
are much mistaken: they are still very much alive
within us! Perhaps you will say, 'But there's no
room in a human being for those huge animals!'

No, of course not, but they are there nevertheless, in another form, in our astral and lower mental bodies. You have to realize that it is neither the physical form nor the size of the animal that counts in this case, it is its nature, the quintessence of its manifestations.

You have almost certainly noticed that, quite apart from its physical appearance, every animal is known for some particular quality or characteristic. A rabbit, for instance, is known not so much for the way it eats or its long, floppy ears, but for the fact that it is easily frightened. If you speak of a wolf you are probably not thinking of its strong, heavy-set neck or the fact that it can run great distances without tiring, but of its killer instinct: when it gets into a sheepfold it is not content to kill just one sheep which would be quite enough to satisfy its appetite, it often strangles several. The lion is known for its pride and courage; the tiger for its cruelty; the eagle for its piercing eye-sight and its love of great heights. The pig is known for its filth; the dog for its faithfulness; the lamb for its gentleness; the cat for its independence and its litheness. The ox is known for its patience; the camel for the frugality of its needs; the cock for its fighting spirit, and so on. The list goes on and on.

The animals are present inside us, therefore, through the presence of their good or bad qualities. And, as I am sure you have noticed, some people's faces are remarkably like the faces of certain animals. Time and again I have had occasion to confirm the observations of the Swiss physiognomist Lavater who remarked on the resemblance between certain human beings and certain animals: pigs, rams, monkeys, dogs, horses, camels, hens, fish, etc.

Watch yourselves closely and I am sure you will find all kinds of animals inside you: a particular attitude or emotion is a lion, another is a scorpion, and so on. Thoughts correspond to winged creatures; there is an analogy between thoughts and birds, whereas feelings cover a much broader field: reptiles, quadrupeds and human beings, as well as elementals, larvae and disembodied spirits. All the tribes or human groups that have ever existed, exist still: none of them has disappeared. They are still alive in man, although it is difficult for you to understand how and in what state of matter these forms remain with us today. For the moment I shall not say more than this on the subject, but remember that everything is contained in man: mountains, lakes, rivers, oceans, swamps, trees, flowers, crystals, minerals, metals and, of course, animals.

And now, what is man's role? Man's mission is to tame, harmonize and reconcile all things in himself. In this way the wild beasts will become domesticated and he can get them to work for him. This is where man's interest lies, as one can see from examples in everyday life: a farmer who has a lot of domestic animals uses them to till the soil and pull heavy loads, and he becomes rich thanks to their work.

Human beings have an immensely important role to play in the plan of creation, but since they have strayed so far from the Fountainhead they have forgotten all about it. They no longer know what role the Lord has destined them for, and instead of educating the animals within them they behave like animals themselves and prey on and devour each other. The only sign of anything truly human can be seen in their houses, their clothes and ornaments, and in some of their books and works of art. Yes, in these things there is some sign of culture. But if you look into the inner life of men, what do you see? A seething mass of all kinds of ferocious beasts, with the very same instincts, the same appetites, the same cruelty. Don't delude yourself into thinking that man has freed himself of his animals. He can't see them, so he thinks they are not there, in his thoughts and feelings. But they are there: very much so! Jealousy, hatred, the desire for revenge — all these are wild animals. And our work, now, is to subdue and tame them and get them to work for us. Anger, vanity, the sexual impulse, all have to be domesticated and harnessed so that we can use them for good. He who learns how to tame his own wild animals can count on their labours and live in plenty, thanks to their collaboration.

We can take the example from what we see in certain parts of the world where there are still wild animals roaming about: if the children, the chickens and the livestock are not protected, the beasts of prey can break in and devour them. Similarly, if men don't learn to defend themselves, wild beasts are liable to raid them and devour their children. But, what children am I talking about? A man's children are all the good thoughts, feelings and acts, all the lovely inspirations that he has given birth to. If he does nothing to protect them they will be devoured by others, by all those hostile forces lying in wait, ready to plunder his henhouse and stables and devour his children. And then he wonders why he is so poverty-stricken, so weak and unsuccessful. Time and time again I have seen this: someone comes to see me, saying, 'I was full of good intentions, but they've all disappeared. I've lost all enthusiasm, all inspiration...' I would love to tell him that it is because he has not been vigilant, because he dozed instead of keeping watch, and the wild beasts got in and destroyed everything, but very often I don't say it because I know he wouldn't believe me. But how else can one explain the fact that all his good intentions have disappeared?

This question of the animals that live within man is very important. In order to master them we have to be strong, and that strength can only come from purity and love. In India, for example, there are many ascetics and yogis who have retired into the jungles to live, and they are not troubled by the wild animals all around them. Animals are very sensitive, much more so than human beings who have lost the power to sense invisible reality. But animals can sense the aura, the light which radiates from a human being. So, if you want to gain the mastery of your inner animals you have to increase the intensity of the light and love within you, in other words, you have to draw nearer to the Lord. Then your animals will begin to feel that you have regained mastery over them and they will be forced to obey you. There is no other way of winning their submission and obedience.

I am not the only one to discover this: thousands of people before me have known that animals obey those who tread the path of light. But the animals I am talking about are those within us. The others are far less important, for not many people are going to have the opportunity to take a stroll through a jungle infested with wild beasts! When I was in India I visited a few places where I was told there were tigers. I was warned to be careful but the extraordinary thing is that I didn't see even one. I wonder why. Perhaps they were afraid of me because they sensed that I was even more ferocious than they, so they kept out of my way. Or perhaps I wasn't given the chance because I hadn't deserved it. Whatever the reason, I still don't know if I would be capable of subduing a wild beast if I met one in the forest!

In the days when Christians were persecuted and thrown to the wild beasts in the arenas, there were cases where the lions refused to touch certain victims, whilst others were immediately torn limb from limb. But this does not necessarily mean that those who were devoured were impure or lacked faith; it simply means that they were predestined to die in that way. For, as you know, the kind of death a man dies is never a question of chance: whether it be from snakebite or the roof of his house collapsing on top of him, whether it be by boiling water, poison, drowning or a wound from a bullet or a knife, the cause of death is always determined beforehand for very precise reasons. Each human being has a special link with one of the elements and it is this link which determines which element — fire, air, water or earth — is to be the agent of his death.

Taming one's own inner animals is a very worthwhile undertaking, and success brings great rewards. If we succeed in taming our inner animals, we shall be capable of taming the animals around us. One can never compel others if one has not first compelled oneself. I have witnessed many lion-tamers at work in various countries, but the fact that they manage to control the circus lions or tigers does not mean that they have mastered the wild beasts within themselves. Their training techniques are based on fear, and the animals obey them because they cannot do otherwise : that's all. The instant the trainer relaxes and lets his guard down the animals pounce on him.

Once, when I was a secondary-school student at Varna in Bulgaria, a snake-charmer came to give us a demonstration of his skills. He was clothed from head to foot in yellow and had bags full of all kinds of snakes, some of them poisonous. He shook some of the snakes out of his bag onto the stage in front of him and began to stare at them intently, and the look in his eye was so formidable that the snakes recoiled from him. We were very impressed, but not long after we learned that he had died : he had been bitten by one of his snakes. Obviously he had not been careful enough. If he had kept a strict watch on himself, if he had controlled and dominated himself and, above all, if he had radiated the love which subdues even the most ferocious animals, he would never have been bitten.

But let's leave that for the moment. Just keep in mind that all the realms of nature exist within us. Our bone structure corresponds to the mineral kingdom; our circulatory system corresponds to the animal kingdom, and our nervous system corresponds to the realm of human beings. Subtler still than the nervous system is the aural system, which represents the frontier between the realms of men and of angels.

All initiatic teachings are unanimous on this score: man is a replica in miniature of the universe. He is known as the *microcosmos* or 'little world', a reflection and synthesis of the *macrocosmos,* the 'greater world'. It is this truth which explains the way in which Initiates work: knowing that every sphere of the created universe exists within themselves, they understand that by setting certain things in motion in their innermost selves they will be touching something in Heaven itself. But unfortunately, although man possesses Heaven within himself, he also possesses Hell. Yes, the Devil and his angels are all there, too. Fortunately they are numb and half-paralysed with cold, and some of them never stir, but if you arouse them as one might arouse a snake, for example, then you will be bitten immediately. If you want to render a snake harmless you have to chill it; it is only dangerous when it is heated.

There are different kinds of heat, and one of them is particularly conducive to arousing the sleeping snake, the serpent of sexual energy. People are always getting bitten because they have overheated this serpent! This is why Initiates endeavour to cool it down: to render it harmless. Now do you see how useful it is to be cool? We have to be cool in this respect and, at the same time, make sure of safeguarding another kind of warmth, the warmth of the heart. Isn't Nature's language extraordinary? And how does one heat the serpent? Well, you don't need me to teach you anything about that. People know all too well how to do it: with alcohol, aphrodisiacs, certain words, looks or gestures, certain perfumes, certain kinds of music. This is how the serpent is aroused and the first thing it does once it is awake is to bite the person who was so rash as to disturb it!

The serpent — or dragon — is within us, but then so is the dove, and there is no love lost between the two. The serpent hates the dove and the dove fears the serpent. I have already explained how, from the astrological point of view, the eagle (the dove) is identified with Scorpio (the serpent), and you certainly remember that the four sacred Animals, the lion, the ox, the eagle and the man, correspond to the four zodiacal signs of Leo, Taurus, Scorpio and Aquarius. And why does the eagle correspond to Scorpio? Because, in the past, it was the eagle who had that position in the Zodiac, but since the Fall of man, Scorpio, which symbolizes the fallen eagle, has taken its place. And now the Scorpio has to become both eagle and dove. In this symbol is contained the whole process of the sublimation of sexual energy.

5

FEAR

There are circumstances in life in which instinct is an excellent guide and others where it is just the reverse. When man was still in a very primitive phase of his evolution, not far removed from the animals, instinct was his most reliable guide, but once his brain developed and he rose to a higher level, he began to need other guides: the guides of reason and intelligence, and today it is these that he must follow. Many things that were acceptable and even good in the past are no longer so, and one example of this is fear. For an animal, fear is a guide to be trusted: fear can save an animal from danger and teach it a great deal. But man can no longer be guided by fear, and that is why the role of Initiation has always been to teach the candidates to conquer fear. The terrifying ordeals to which disciples in the ancient sanctuaries of Initiation were subjected, often had no other goal than to force them to overcome the fear inherited from the animal kingdom.

No better remedy than love has ever been found for fear. If you love you no longer fear. Knowledge is very effective also, but not always as effective as love, because love, like fear, springs from the instinctual dimension and one instinct is more easily defeated by another than by knowledge or reason. There are times when reason can calm one's fears, but the effects are not always long-lasting or very reliable, whereas if you touch someone's heart he will go through fire for you ! Take the example of a woman who sees a stranger in danger : not knowing him she would hesitate to risk her life to save him, but if it were her own child who was in danger she would not hesitate : without a second thought she would rush to his rescue. Or take the case of a young girl who was too fearful to walk through a graveyard alone at night : if she had to do so to meet her beloved she would not hesitate. Only love can give such courage.

In other instances, it is true, knowledge can be an effective weapon against fear. Suppose you have lost your way in the middle of a forest : you don't know which path to take and, naturally, you are frightened. But if you have a compass or a flashlight and know which direction you should take, then you have no need to be afraid. Man is always afraid of something he does not understand or know how to use, just as animals fear fire or, in the past, primitive men trembled before the forces of nature. Now that men have tamed these forces they can work in electric or nuclear power stations and throw this switch or turn on that tap without a tremor, because they know what they are doing. But someone who did not know what all those switches and levers were about would be afraid to touch anything.

Cultured, civilized man, therefore, is no longer afraid of the elements or of the forces of nature. No, but he is afraid of his wife, his neighbour or his boss; he is afraid of illness, poverty and death and, above all, he is afraid of public opinion! He may fear neither God nor the Devil, but he trembles before public opinion and is ready to sacrifice everything rather than offend it. Civilized man still has many unconquered fears, for the instinct of fear is deeply rooted in the human soul, and it takes a very long time to vanquish it. Fear can take many different forms, and when it is driven out of one area of our lives it sneaks in to another.

Nastradine Hodja* who was no fool, had noticed that, although they would not admit it, everyone was afraid of something. One day, finding

* Known in English as Mullah Nashrudin.

himself without a penny to his name, he decided he would make his fortune by forcing people to admit that they were afraid of something. He went to see the Sultan, and said, 'May the blessings of Allah be on your head! I have come to beg a favour of you: grant me permission to demand one penny from every one of your subjects who is afraid of something.' 'That's not much to ask,' said the Sultan; 'Request granted!' Some time went by, and Nastradine Hodja returned from his travels leading three camels loaded with the coins he had collected, for, one way or another, all those he had met on his way had revealed either by their words or their attitudes that they were afraid of something or someone. Nastradine Hodja appeared before the Sultan and said, 'Everybody was obliged to give me a penny; not one man did I meet who was not forced to admit that he was afraid of something. And now I have come to collect a penny from you, too!' 'Ho, ho!' said the Sultan; 'You'll have to go away empty-handed, for I am afraid of nothing!' However, the Sultan was a generous man and he invited Nastradine Hodja to eat and drink with him and some of his concubines. In the middle of the banquet, Nastradine Hodja, who was sitting next to the Sultan, said in a loud voice, 'Majesty, I met the most beautiful woman on my journey. You have been very kind to me and enabled me to become rich and I want to thank you by giving you this woman. She is really worthy of gracing your harem. If you like, I'll go and bring her to you.' 'Shh!' exclaimed the Sultan; 'Not so loud, my favourite concubine will hear..' 'Ah, you see, Majesty. You are afraid of something: give me my penny!'

Perhaps you will say, 'But is it so important not to be afraid of anything? One can live perfectly well even if one is afraid!' That is true, of course, but suppose you come across a fierce dog in the street: if you are frightened and start to run away, it will sense your fear and run after you, barking. And if other dogs see their friend chasing you they will join in and start barking and chasing after you too. So, there you are, with a whole pack of dogs on your heels all because you were afraid of one of them! If, instead of being afraid and running away, you had turned on the dog and ordered it to keep quiet it would not have bothered you.

In any case, speaking in general, if ever you find yourself in some kind of danger, before reacting in any way, stay absolutely quiet for an instant. Don't move, don't say a word; clench your right fist and take a deep breath and unite yourself to the Lord, and in this way you will be in control of your cells. Then do whatever you have to do to escape the danger, but always begin by staying absolutely still. If you move at once you will be releasing a dam and the flood waters will sweep everything away beyond your control. You can see examples of this when people panic and jump from a top-storey window or dash into a burning building.

In the face of danger you must remain motionless for an instant and unite yourself with Providence. If you do this you will feel that peace is taking control, and it is this peace which is the primary condition for the mobilisation of beneficial forces dormant within you. You will feel them springing into action and witness their power; they are always there, within you, but conditions have to be right for them to manifest themselves.

This law holds good both for the internal and the external worlds. When you feel that you are being threatened from within, don't 'run away' otherwise your enemy will simply chase after you and the faster you run the more you will be pursued and bitten. React as you would with a dog: turn and look at the monsters who are trying to terrify you; stare them in the face and they will turn tail and run. But this is just what you are unable to do: instead of facing up to danger you run for help from the chemist or your psychiatrist! Well, that is the very best way to ensure that these creatures will go on persecuting you, for you must also realize that there is a law according to which, if you fear something you are creating the perfect conditions for that thing to occur. If you do not want to attract misfortune, therefore, begin by not being afraid of it. As soon as you show yourself to be strong you will be left in peace.

If, for example, a man is afraid to look at a nude woman because he is afraid of being tempted and losing control of himself (I know that this particular fear is less and less frequent; on the contrary, people are eager for temptation to come their way! But we'll take the example all the same); well, it is this fear that creates conditions conducive to his fall. What is so bad about seeing a nude woman? There is nothing evil there; the evil lies in being weak and giving way to temptation. One must not be weak, that's all! One must not give way to temptation and then excuse oneself by declaring that one couldn't help it! Anyone who says that temptation was too strong for him is signing his own death warrant: nothing must be too strong for you.

So many people take refuge in that excuse: 'I couldn't help it. The temptation was too strong.' And everybody finds that normal, of course, because the weak understand each other. But an Initiate would simply say, 'There goes an ignorant, weak-willed man who will always be up against things that are too strong for him. Whether it be anger or sensuality, jealousy or the desire for revenge, there will always be something that defeats him!' But when will you begin to get the upper hand? If you don't begin now, in this incarnation, to make an effort and to get the better of some of your weaknesses, you will be no further forward in the next incarnation.

Human beings are at the mercy of their own fears without realizing that they come from a lack of knowledge, a lack of light. Do you want proof of that? When you go into a dark house and you don't know your way about, you only begin to feel safe when you have lit a lamp. What fantastic conclusions one can draw from this phenomenon for one's spiritual life! Darkness is ignorance, and because we sense that there is danger in darkness we are afraid.

If you examine the question more closely, you will see that even the moral laws that have been given to man are based on fear: the fear that he will give in to his weaknesses. For one who is strong and in perfect control of himself, everything is right, everything is permitted. But where the weak are concerned one has to take precautions: even Heaven is closed to them, for Heaven would drive them mad! Just think about it, when you are weak everything is dangerous: love, beauty, purity, light, joy. It is dangerous just to be alive! So what is left? Nothing! How many rules and regulations have been invented just because of human weakness! But as soon as man is stronger, things which are forbidden to him now will be recommended. When there is no longer any reason for the existence of certain moral rules they will be done away with.

When men no longer steal or commit adultery, why should they have to listen to commandments against such things? And in fact I must tell you that marriage was invented when love began to disappear: since human beings no longer knew what true love was they had to be bound by a contract. In the natural order of things it is love which determines the existence of marriage. Nature recognizes no other. For society, if you have not pronounced your vows in church or in a registry office you are not married, but Nature does not recognize that as marriage, she only recognizes love. This is so true, you know! The institution of marriage exists, but does that prevent people from separating? No, love is the only thing that can keep them together.

I told you that love was your best weapon against fear and I gave you some examples. But now I must add that it is only love for our Creator, love for Him who maintains and controls everything, for Him who distributes all gifts, the richest, the most beautiful and the most powerful Being — it is only when we love Him that we begin to feel protected. And once we feel protected we have no more fear : this is an important psychological law. But psychologists are far more interested in illnesses and deviations than in attitudes which enable men to triumph in all the circumstances of their lives. Take the example of those who have accepted martyrdom for their faith, for an ideal: where did they get the strength? And why should you spend your life trembling for the least little thing? Suppose you know someone who is very rich : look how he struts about, how he fires off orders, how he always expects to have his own way! But take away all his money and what do you see? He is a deflated balloon, on the verge of suicide, and all because he no longer feels the protection of his wealth. So all his might was in his money : he himself was neither strong nor powerful.

The Gospels say that they who are afraid will not enter into the Kingdom of Heaven. This is a sure indication of how important it is for a disciple to conquer fear. He may have all kinds of other qualities and virtues, but if he is afraid his other virtues cannot guarantee that he will be admitted into the Kingdom of God. Does that surprise you? It shouldn't. How often one sees that fear prevents all kinds of good qualities from manifesting themselves. Have you never seen how the fear of solitude, poverty, dishonour, illness and death can make people cowardly, dishonest, egotistical and cruel? How many crimes are committed because people cling to something they love and are afraid of losing it! In ancient times, candidates asking for Initiation had to face ordeals in which they could prove that they had conquered fear. And we, too, have to conquer fear, knowing that hidden behind all the trials and difficulties that await us, behind all the dangers that threaten us, is God Himself. Yes, God is hidden in each one of the trials sent to teach us something. This is why, if we want to rid ourselves of all fear, we must learn to forget ourselves completely and take refuge in the consciousness of our union with God.

If it is ordained that you must die, where can you go to escape? People have been known to travel great distances in order to find a safe refuge, and just as they reached their destination death caught up with them in a totally unexpected way. Instead of being afraid we should tell ourselves that we are in God's hands and that whatever happens to us is His concern. If He finds that we are useful to Him, here, He will save us, otherwise we shall have to go. It is pointless to think we can preserve our own life, it does not belong to us, it belongs to God. Fear comes from our ignorance of this. So this is why, in order to conquer fear, we must consecrate our life to God so that He may do what He wishes with it. The only fear that is allowed us then, indeed the one fear that we must have, is the fear of transgressing the Divine Law. He who has lost this fear is, himself, lost: he is in danger from all sides. The fear of transgressing the laws of God is a very healthy sentiment which should always be present in our soul.

From now on, therefore, whenever you find yourself faced with something difficult, instead of being afraid and running away, try to face up to the enemy, otherwise it will never let go of you. In order to conquer our enemies on the astral and mental planes we need boldness and courage; in other words we need both light and warmth, because light (knowledge) and warmth (love) combined, produce the strength which enables us to triumph.

6

STEREOTYPES

If you ask a biologist to explain heredity to you, he will tell you that all the character traits with which a child is born were contained in his parents chromosomes, and that if one could modify the chromosomes one would be in a position to influence a child's character. It is quite true that the chromosomes contain all the elements needed to determine the characteristics of a child, but chromosomes are only the biochemical aspect of the question.

Esoteric science teaches that everything on earth has its double. Even our physical body has its double (this is what we know as the etheric body), and although it is made of a different, far more subtle matter, the form and functions of the etheric body are exactly the same as those of the physical body. Our etheric body is the seat of the memory. It is this body which has the power to record and preserve all the events and circumstances exterior to ourselves, as well as all our own thoughts, feelings and desires. The records preserved by the etheric body are comparable to a photographic negative or stereotype from which thousands of identical copies can be made. Once something has been recorded — whether it be a thought, a feeling or an act — it must necessarily repeat itself over and over again. And this is how habits are born. If you want to change a habit you have to change your negative or stereotype.

But you will understand this better if I give you an example. Take a seed, for instance: it is a stereotype. The lines of force that are going to determine the characteristics of the plant as it grows are, of course, invisible, but if you plant the seed and keep it watered, and if the sun warms it in the ground, before long you will see a tiny shoot and the first fragile stem and leaves thrusting out of the soil. The blueprints for the growth and development of the plant were already stored in the seed by the most intelligent of beings. How could one explain the perfection of proportions and the beauty of every plant if the seed did not contain a secret stereotype containing the lines of force necessary to channel its energies and guide its growth? Similarly, if certain human beings are constantly driven to commit the same crime, it is because they have a stereotype within them which, like the lines of force of a plant, guides them according to a predetermined pattern. In the beginning — no one knows when : it may have been in this life or in a previous incarnation — they must have entertained a thought or feeling or committed an act which was etched into the etheric material of the brain in the form of a stereotype. Once the stereotype exists they continue to repeat the same gestures, to entertain the same thoughts or feelings, because nature is faithful and steadfast ; she never forgets. This is why I say that the chromosomes are not sufficient to explain the temperament of a child : its origins are more remote than that. But biologists have never studied these questions from the initiatic point of view, so they are unaware that the etheric body has its stereotypes which come from previous lives, and that these stereotypes are far more important than chromosomes.

Take another example, if you like, from everyday life : the case of someone who is learning the piano. If he fails to take into account the law of etheric records, he will begin to practise a new piece rapidly and perhaps a bit carelessly. And, of course, because he is going too fast and not paying enough attention to what he is doing, he is bound to make at least one mistake and probably more ! And once those mistakes have been recorded in his subconscious it is too late : he

cannot rub them out. Twenty or thirty years later,
even if he knows the piece by heart, every time he
comes to the spot where he made his first mistake
he has to be particularly careful, otherwise he
would make the same mistake again: the stereotype is still there. So I advise musicians always to
begin practising a new piece of music without
hurrying, note by note, taking all the time they
need to cut a perfect stereotype. If they start
slowly and carefully, later they can go as fast as
they please, extremely fast, without ever making a
mistake because the stereotype in their subconscious is note perfect.

This is an infallible law. If you fail to apply it
you will be obliged to begin over and over again,
five times, ten times and more — and even then
the problem will not be solved. You will always
have to take special care in order not to fall into
the same old mistakes and that means a lot of
wasted effort. Whereas with a little wisdom and
intelligence you can economize both time and
energy. Never go at something in a hurry: work
slowly and with great care so as to cut a perfect
stereotype. Have you ever seen an engraver at
work? If he is tense or in a hurry and his tool slips
as he is working, even though the mistake may be
very slight, the damage is done once and for all
and it can't be undone. It is engraved into the
metal. But human beings are not good psycholo-

gists, they rush at things — or at other people — without paying attention, with no concern for precision and no sensitivity for the person or thing concerned, and in this way they make all kinds of mistakes which they repeat time after time all their lives long. Once they realize that they have blundered, of course, they try to repair the damage, but it can't be done. They go on and on making the same silly mistakes, committing the same faults and indulging the same vices, for the law is applicable in every domain. Suppose a man begins smoking, running after girls or helping himself from other people's pockets: at once the stereotype is engraved in the memory of his cells and he will repeat the same gestures for ever. It is like printing: if you don't change the type in the press you will go on printing the same text.

Once one knows about these things one can avoid many sorrows and disappointments and a great deal of bitterness. But human beings who have no instructor think they have the right to do just about anything, and they don't realize that it is all recorded, all engraved in their subconscious. Nature records everything; everything is faithfully remembered. People say, 'I'll do thus and so just this once. Never again!' Yes, but once it is done it is on record. The stereotype is there, and leads to their doing it a second and then a third, and any number of times again. This is why I

strongly advise against launching into all kinds
of risky undertakings on the pretext of wanting to
experience everything at least once. This is the
fashion, nowadays, particularly amongst young
people: they want to try everything, taste everything, experience every sensation. And so they
plunge headlong into a whirl of pleasure and passion, wild behaviour, drugs, violence, unbridled
sexual activity, etc., etc. Yes, but once the stereotype is cut, even if they want to mend their ways
and live another kind of life, they find themselves
incapable of doing so — and that's the tragedy of
it!

However, there is a way to escape from the
domination of your old stereotypes and it is
extremely simple: you have to prepare new ones,
by adopting a new attitude, cultivating new
thoughts and feelings and acquiring new habits.
In this way you will be making new recordings,
new stereotypes to take the place of the old ones.

Take the example of a train: whatever you try
to do about it, it will always run on the rails on
which it has started. If you want it to go in a
different direction you will have to lay down new
rails. Well, stereotypes are railway lines and the
disciple has to lay down new ones within himself.
In other words, he has to give himself other ideals
and cultivate other tendencies, other interests. If
he doesn't know how to do this he can talk as

much as he likes about changing his ways and doing better : 'I'm going to change. I'm going to mend my ways and live a better life. I'll do better next time!', since he has not actually done anything to change and improve, when 'next time' comes along it will be just as bad as the last time, and his train will continue to run along the same old lines. The best way is to say nothing to anybody and to change the direction of your rails. In other words, put new stereotypes in the place of the old ones, and your train will be bound to go a different way. But there is one thing you have to understand : when you cut a new stereotype it does not mean that the old one has disappeared. No, it never disappears, it is only filed away in the archives of your subconscious, buried under layers of other records. If you want it to remain buried you have to be extremely watchful, always on your guard; as soon as you relax your vigilance the old stereotype will come up to the surface again.

You must realize that nothing that has once existed ever ceases to exist. Nothing ever disappears completely because Cosmic Intelligence is determined to keep a full record of everything in its archives, every detail of the History of the world, everything that has happened in the billions of years that the world has existed has been carefully preserved. What makes you think that human beings are the only ones to keep archives? If Nature didn't keep a complete record of everything that occurs in the universe, her work would be greatly hindered.

Even your work might be hindered: isn't it possible that, in the course of your evolution, you might need to consult the records of your past lives? And how could you do so if everything had been obliterated and there was no mention of them in any record? In fact, nothing is ever obliterated, and if you manage to gain admittance to these archives one day you will be able to read the story of your past: the different countries in which you lived, your different identities, all the good you have ever done as well as all your crimes. And when you see all that you will understand how the Law of Karma applies to you and why your present circumstances are as they are. If the great Initiates are in a position to reveal their teaching of Divine Justice, it is precisely because they have studied these records. And you can study them, too, and you will come to the same conclusions. The path is always there — it only remains to follow it!

Some people can never get away from certain persistent thoughts and feelings which pursue them like an angry swarm of wasps. It would take quite a long time to explain this fully. Space is filled with countless forces, currents and entities created by those who inhabit it. Some of these creations are extremely beautiful, but others are hideously ugly and when they find that somebody has left their door open they rush in. If you are not very careful and attentive, if you have cut your ties with the regions of sublime beauty and left your mind, heart and soul open to all the vagabonds of space, you will often be bothered by them. But if, on the contrary, you have learned how to prepare yourself inwardly you can make sure that you attract only beneficial influences which will accompany you wherever you go, bringing you endless inspiration and delight.

Perhaps you will ask, 'But, are thoughts and feelings the same thing as stereotypes?' No. Thoughts and feelings are not, themselves, stereotypes, rather they are forces which have been attracted by certain stereotypes. It is our attitudes and habits which are the stereotypes, and it is they that determine the kind of influences that are drawn to us. If our stereotypes are truly beautiful, the images reflected on our screen will also be beautiful, but if our stereotypes are hideous and deformed, then obviously the results will not be too wonderful. If you wear a talisman charged with good, beneficial forces, it will attract forces and currents of the same kind. But if someone puts an evil talisman on your doorstep, for instance, it will bring all kinds of misfortunes on the people in your house. Unfortunately, some human beings wear evil 'talismans' within themselves, talismans that they have prepared and charged with negative forces through their own ignorance and vice and which continue to attract evil influences.

If you want to change your destiny you have to change your stereotypes; you have to exert yourselves in order to acquire new habits and new attitudes and cover up and bury your old stereotypes under the new ones. Just as an example, take the case of someone who decides he must stop slandering his neighbour, or that he must cure himself of his uncontrollable temper. If he has not thought of changing his stereotypes, at the first opportunity he will slide back into his old habit. Full of remorse and disappointment with himself, he will be utterly miserable and swear that next time things will be different. But when the next time comes along things are exactly the same as before. If he really wants it to be different he is going to have to change something in what he does and the way he does it, and if he can succeed just once then he has a good chance of succeeding again, next time, and the time after, for every time he succeeds the new stereotype is etched more deeply. We can apply this system to rid ourselves of all the deplorable, negative habits and tendencies that plague us: dishonesty, sensuality, greed, laziness and so on. Once you have managed to engrave the ideal stereotype within you, you can sleep in peace because you can rely on it to attract all the most marvellous forces and currents from the outermost limits of the universe. As soon as they see the brand new stereotypes that have replaced your old ones they set out in your direction. Yes, but you have to be patient, because they have millions of miles to come and it may take them a long time to reach you!

Man's destiny is written in the stereotypes he brings with him when he is born on this earth. When you see a tiny baby you marvel at how innocent and guileless it seems, but if you could see the stereotypes some babies are born with, and the appalling things their stereotypes are going to make them do later on, once they begin to take effect, you might not be so full of admiration! Each one of us comes into this world with the stereotypes he has prepared for himself in his previous incarnation, and the thoughts and feelings that plague him are simply the consequences of those stereotypes. But if someone has prepared good stereotypes he will be inaccessible to evil influences, whatever his circumstances. He may feel evil forces and currents all round him but they will be powerless to penetrate his defences.

Now, let me give you yet another method : when you are besieged by negative thoughts and feelings which refuse to leave you in peace in spite of your best efforts, remember that if you cannot get rid of them it is because you have not been working on your new stereotypes long enough to ensure immediate results. In this case, what should you do ? The best thing to do is to assume the attitude of an onlooker : step back, as it were, and stare at all those negative, malevolent entities and forces which are trying to break in to your stronghold. Watch the tricks they get up to and all the different ways they try to fool you. In this way, by observing them from a distance, you have already shown that you are capable of getting above them, and they begin to feel very uncomfortable under your steady gaze. They don't like to be watched. And, above all, if you focus a ray of light onto them they will scatter in all directions because they can't bear light ! They may well come back again. In fact they are bound to come back again until your new stereotypes are securely in place. But every time they come back, if you repeat the same procedure : gaze steadily at them and focus a beam of light onto them, you will end by getting rid of them for good. Yes, simply because you managed to keep above them. That is the secret of this method.

This is one of the laws of life: someone who is above others, the head, the person in charge, has the right to command, to threaten, to give orders. Even if the king is insane, he has the right to send his entire army into the field, simply because of his rank: he is their superior. So you, too, if you rise above these troublesome entities they will be obliged to obey you.

There! Now you have several methods at your disposal. From now on, therefore, instead of weeping and lamenting and tearing your hair out, use the methods I have given you. Obviously, the most effective one is to change your stereotypes, but it takes longer and requires greater efforts than the others.

How much there is to learn! Life is so vast, so immensely rich, we still have no notion of what it really is. And this is why an Initiatic school is needed, so that we can learn what to do and how to do it in this life: how to get help from a particular benevolent force or, on the contrary, how to disarm and banish antagonistic forces. Only when you are capable of doing this will you really and truly find fulfilment.

7

GRAFTING

A science exists which makes it possible for one who has studied it, not only to correct and control his faults, passions and baser tendencies, but even to use them to his advantage. This is the science of grafting.

As you know, fruit-farmers have developed this technique in order to improve the quality of the fruit they grow. For instance, they can graft a slip from a cultivated pear tree which gives sweet, succulent fruit, onto the stock of a wild pear tree which, although it is healthy and vigorous, produces only hard, inedible fruit. The cutting will benefit from the vigour of the wild tree and produce delicious, juicy pears. But if you want to become expert in this art, you have to know certain laws of nature, for you cannot graft any and every kind of cutting onto stock that is incompatible. Even with fruit trees there are certain affinities and correspondences: you cannot graft a cutting from a tree which produces fruit with pips; apples for instance, onto a plum tree or other tree which produces fruit with stones.

Human beings have become pastmasters in techniques of this kind, but when it comes to the psychic or spiritual domain they are not nearly so capable or ingenious. One sees so many distinguished people: scientists, famous writers and artists, philosophers and statesmen, all in the grip of some vice or passion and incapable of freeing themselves from it. So many artists of talent — of genius even — drank, took drugs or ruined themselves at the gaming tables or with women! There is no point in telling you their names, but they have all gone to the grave with their weaknesses still intact. If they had only known the rules for making grafts they could have grafted all kinds of qualities and virtues onto their weaknesses.

Now, how is this done? Suppose, for instance, that you have a very loving nature, but that your love is very sensual. You can look on it as a great strength; a tall, vigorous tree whose energies can be harnessed and used to nourish and strengthen a cutting grafted onto it from another kind of love, one that is pure, noble and disinterested. The sap produced by your lower nature will rise and circulate through the new branches, that is, through these new stereotypes, the new circuits etched into your brain, producing magnificent fruit, the fruit of a prodigious love which will enrapture and inspire you in ways you never thought possible. Instead of making life unbearable for you, your sensuality will become a generous reservoir of forces capable of raising you all the way to the Divine Mother and the Heavenly Father.

Or perhaps it is your overweening vanity which absorbs all your energies: there, too, you can do a graft. If you decide to give up your ambition of being great and glorious in the eyes of the world, in the eyes of gossips and gawking idiots, and put your vanity at the service of an ideal by grafting a spiritual ambition onto it, it will become a driving force urging you towards a Heavenly goal, and one day you will find that your vanity has been transformed into divine glory.

If you have a violent temper it is more than likely that, in a fit of anger, you have already destroyed more than one friendship and spoiled your chances of future promotion. Well, instead of letting the blind force of your anger explode like a thunderbolt, you can do a graft and transform and sublimate it. If you do this you will be tireless in the battle against all your weaknesses and evil tendencies; you will become a valiant servant of God, an invincible soldier of Christ. Instead of creating havoc and laying waste all around you, your Martian energies

can be used to build something positive. All
you have to do is find a cutting to graft onto
them.

So stereotypes and grafts are two different
methods which you must learn to use. Old stereotypes have to be replaced by new ones, but grafts
are different: they simply have to be added on to
what is already there. If you want to graft a cutting you have to be sure that the roots are still
there and in good health. You must never attempt
to tear them out, for both roots and trunk are
vigorous and full of life, and the new shoots you
graft onto them are going to need their energies.
These wild, untamed forces can be diverted to the
service of a higher entity, a Spirit of light, an
Angel or an Archangel. Do you see, now, what I
mean by a graft? All the great Initiates have had
to perform grafts in order to bear sweeter, more
flavourful fruits, and they did this by allying
themselves with the most exalted, sublime Beings.

You may say, 'I have read about such and
such a hero, saint or prophet who lived in the
past, and I find his life tremendously inspiring. I
have great admiration for him. Do you think he
could provide me with a graft?' It is quite possible. The only trouble is that as someone like that
existed a long time ago, you cannot be in such
close touch with him and talk to him as you can
with a living being. In fact, even if you choose a

human being who is still alive — a friend, a renowned philosopher or artist, for instance — and whom you admire greatly, the graft would still be somewhat imperfect, because everybody has some weakness or defect. None of them is absolutely strong, luminous, powerful, warm and generous.

Ah, but there is someone who is infinitely more intelligent, more loving, more powerful and more generous than anyone you could ever find on earth, and who has a storehouse full of cuttings which are ideal for the grafts you need: and that being is the sun! He is the one you have to go to for your cuttings. From now on, when you are in front of the rising sun, speak to him and ask him for the grafts you need: 'Oh, Sun, my friend, there are so many things I'd love to understand, but my intelligence is so limited. But you who are all light, you who give light to the whole world, I know how generous you are: please give me a few little cuttings from your immense intelligence!' And he will, you know! He'll give them to you free of charge, and you can graft them into your brain. In fact, if you are not sure how to set about it, he will even send you an expert to help you! Then you can ask him for other cuttings: kindness, beauty or wisdom, for example. You can ask him for all the cuttings you need; he has them all. But don't ask for them all at the same time, you

would not be able to graft them all at once and
some of them would wither and die from lack of
attention. Ask for them one by one.

Several of you are wondering if I'm making
fun of you: and the answer is, 'No, absolutely
not!' I am perfectly serious about this for I have
used these methods myself, for years, and I can
assure you that they are very effective. In fact
there are many other things I have not told you
about grafting, but what you don't learn from me
you will learn directly from the sun. Everything I
know has been revealed to me by the sun. You may
be astonished to hear that the sun can reveal
things to human beings, but it is true, nevertheless!

Of course it is possible to use cuttings from a
great Master for your grafts because the light and
warmth (wisdom and love) of a great Master sym-
bolize the light and heat of the sun. But still, no
Master can compare with the sun. True, a human
being can resemble the sun to the extent to which
he spreads warmth, light and life to those who
come near him. But the sun gives light, warmth
and nourishment to the whole world. All life on
earth comes from the sun; every living thing
which grows and reaches maturity does so thanks
to the sun. An Initiate can do some good to
mankind but he can never have such power as
this: no mortal can be compared to the sun.

The sun's rays are capable of doing away with all the shabbiness, all that is worn out and dirty, all the dark, impure elements within you. But if you want this to happen you have to learn how to open yourselves to their action. If you open wide your hearts, the rays of the sun can begin to work on you and get rid of your 'old Adam', and you will find yourself renewed and reborn, as though raised from the dead. Everything will be transformed and transfigured: all your thoughts, feelings and acts will be changed. Unfortunately, many people who enjoy marvellous sensations when they are eating and drinking, smoking or making love, feel nothing at all when they watch the sun rising. This is because their vibrations are at too low a frequency: the lowest kinds of sensations make an impression on them, but sunbeams leave them cold. But once a disciple begins to advance and evolve he becomes more sensitive to the sun's rays and they give him all kinds of revelations and raptures — truly heavenly sensations.

And this, again, is something quite new. Modern psychology has not yet discovered that the power of the sun's rays to produce effects of such tremendous importance in our hearts and souls, effects that can restore our youth and totally regenerate us, depends on our own attitude. But, of course, we have to prepare ourselves

before the sun's rays can have beneficial effects; if
we don't prepare ourselves we shall remain
forever untouched by the sun. For days, and even
weeks and months, we have to prepare ourselves
to be clear-headed and lucid, capable of being
suffused by the suns's rays and of experiencing
their purity and their divine potency.

But the most powerful graft of all, and the
most sublime, is that by which we unite with the
Lord Himself. Say to Him, 'Lord God, I am
worthless. I know it. But enter into me, work in
me, manifest Yourself through me. I only ask to
work for the coming of Your Kingdom and Your
Justice on earth.' If God hears your prayer and
comes to you, your tree — by which I mean you,
yourself — which produced nothing but bitter,
inedible fruit in the past, will soon start producing sweet, succulent fruit. All that remains of
your 'tree' is the roots and the trunk, but the cutting grafted onto it, that is, the Divine, Invisible
World, Heaven itself, produces fruit of its own on
your tree. Perhaps you wonder how this happens? Well, it is simply that when you pledge all
those raw, turbulent energies within you to the
service of the Lord, He accepts them and transforms them. Sometimes, in the woods, one comes
across a wild pear tree, with very small, hard,
inedible fruit. But if you heat those pears in the
oven for a few minutes, they become soft and

sweet : they are transformed by the heat. Well, if man is capable of making wild pears fit to eat, don't you think that the Invisible World is certainly capable of transforming your own sour fruits into sweet, juicy ones?

A disciple who is conscious of his own vile tendencies can ask the Lord to help him to graft a nobler species onto himself : 'Lord God, if You leave me to myself I'll never be any better. Help me. Do whatever You please with me. Use me as Your instrument, I am at Your service, I promise to do Your will.' If you pledge yourself in this way, it may not be the Lord Himself who comes to help you, but He will certainly send someone, an Angel or an Archangel, just as He sent Angels to the Patriarchs, Prophets, Apostles and Saints in the past : they were visited and instructed by Angels.

These are extremely important questions and anyone who neglects them or remains in ignorance of them will never evolve very far. Human beings are hardheaded, but life will take care of them and make those hard heads ripen ! I know what I'm talking about. I never tell you anything that I have not tested and confirmed for myself then, when I have proved its worth, I can help you by revealing it to you. But if you want to get results, you have to feel and understand what I tell you and make up your minds to put it into practice.

As I say, if you don't know these things you can never really improve very much. However, it is not enough to know, you also have to love these great truths; you have to love them and desire with all your heart to put them into effect, and you have to have the undaunted determination to persevere in your efforts. These are the three indispensable conditions for success: knowledge, love or desire, and the power that comes from unswerving resolution.

There are human beings who have transformed themselves so completely that they are not the same creatures. On the outside, of course, there is no apparent change, but inwardly they are quite different. They no longer suffer as they used to, they no longer feel themselves overburdened and hemmed in on every side, they are no longer in perpetual darkness, they have found new inner wealth and new knowledge, and they bathe in an ocean of dazzling splendour, shedding light all around them. This is the kind of change we are talking about! It has nothing to do with changing one's physical appearance. No, if you change in this way, your friends and acquaintances will still recognize you. What counts is to change on the inside, to change your vibrations and emanations; to change in such a way that you can give a glass of water to a dying man and restore him to life simply because you have touched the water with your hand! This is the change we are talking about!

8

THE USE OF ENERGY

Everything that a man's heart could wish for, everything that could possibly exist for the pleasure and amusement of men is all laid out for them to choose from. I admit that many of these things are very interesting and attractive, but that is no reason for me to pounce on them without weighing the pros and cons: on the contrary! Whenever I am faced with something new I am in the habit of asking myself one question: 'Is this something that can help me to advance spiritually?' And when the answer is negative, when I see that, on the contrary, it is more likely to be a waste of time and energy, I put it aside.

Oh, yes! Life is full of all kinds of temptations and if a disciple has not learned sufficient self-control to be able to resist them, he gives way and then, afterwards, he regrets it because he feels weakened and degraded. Most people, of course, find it normal to be tempted and, especially, to give in to temptation; in fact a great many people think that that is why they are on earth! But at the moment I am not concerned about what most people think or do: I am concerned about what a disciple does. A disciple could avoid a great many mistakes if he paused before launching out into any new venture, and asked himself this one question: 'If I do this, that or the other I will be satisfying my appetites, but what effect will it have on me and on those around me?' Someone who never asks himself this kind of question is constantly surprised at what happens to him. But there should be no cause for surprise: whatever happens could have been foreseen. The consequences of our acts are always foreseeable.

You will probably object that it is quite impossible to foresee all the consequences of your acts. That is true: life is full of unexpected events which can completely change our circumstances. Except for those few who have the power to rise to the subtler levels of reality and learn exactly what the future holds, no one can foresee everything. But anyone who is honest and sincere can easily foresee the essential features of the consequences which will result from his acts. Of course, if one wants to blind oneself, that is different.

I repeat, therefore: when you are faced with various possibilities and have to make a choice, study the situation carefully and choose whichever option will be most beneficial for your spiritual progress. It is absolutely essential for your evolution that you know exactly what you spend your energies on and where they go. Each one of us is personally responsible in this respect. Heaven has not given us life so that we can fritter it away: what we do with it is noted and recorded. Yes, and in the book of living Nature it is written: 'Blessed are those who dedicate and use all their energies, physical, emotional and mental, for the good of mankind and for the Kingdom of God and His Justice.'

If you observe human beings closely, you will notice that they never think about this precious quintessence they have been given to spend in living; they never think about how priceless it is, how much importance the Lord attaches to it, where it comes from or how hard Nature has had to work in order to prepare it and distribute it to each one of us. This is the touchstone by which you can see that man is not very highly evolved, for he wastes all his life forces in fits of anger, unrestrained sensuality and criminal, egotistical activities. And this is how all those precious energies go to nourish the forces of Hell. If I told you that it was human beings who supplied Hell with all its energies you would be astounded — and yet that is exactly what happens. The vast majority of human beings are so ignorant that they spend their lives encouraging, supporting and nourishing the forces of Evil. Oh, they know all there is to know in every human science, but they have never heard that they are responsible for the way in which they use their energies — and it is certainly not in any of the universities that they are likely to learn that!

As disciples, your first task is to become aware of how you use your energies, because they have all been counted, weighed and measured and when Heaven sees that you are frittering them away in harmful activities they cut off the supply. They say, 'Look at that one; he's dangerous! He'll have to be tied up.' You don't even know why some people become hopeless drunks! It is because the Invisible World has decided to put them in a strait jacket. If they were in full possession of their faculties they would wreak havoc in the world by putting all their energies into works of destruction, whereas now they are besotted and stupefied by alcohol and they cannot do much damage. Of course, this is not true of all alcoholics; the explanation is quite different for some.

You must always know, always be conscious of how you are using your energies, to what end you are using them. This is the most important of all.

Nowadays, for instance, it has become a habit, a fashion, to be a rebel. Everybody argues and shouts, they take to the streets in protests and strikes, cars are overturned and burned, and everybody thinks they are in the right when they oppose an unjust, tyrannical employer or government. In a way that is true, I agree that one must not accept injustice or cruelty. But what strikes me is that it never seems to have occurred to people who behave like this that there are, perhaps, other more worthwhile targets for revolt. Instead of wasting all their time and energy rebelling against one particular situation, person or political party, why don't they rebel against their own weaknesses, their own mediocrity and laziness? There, at least, they would find something to arouse their indignation and disgust, something really worth fighting against. Oh, no, no! They can always find excuses for their own stupidity and vices, and instead of struggling against them they nourish and indulge them. But when it comes to other people, they know no mercy!

Instead of rising up in revolt against somebody else — a reaction which is usually quite useless, anyway — a true disciple rebels against the evil entities which, through his own fault, of course, have made their home within him. He does all he can to turn them out and free himself from them. If rebellion exists in the universe it is because it has a role to play. The only trouble is that human beings have not understood where, when nor how, nor against whom they should rebel. It is important to be a rebel, yes! But you have to rebel against all those entities who have infiltrated your inner Self in the shape of various weaknesses, and who do nothing but cheat you and nibble away at your reserves. If you rebel against them, then everything becomes different. Many people are keenly aware of their faults and failings and this makes them unhappy and very dissatisfied with themselves. But they have not done what they should to rebel against the situation and to free themselves, so it just goes on and on. They are dissatisfied with the state of affairs but they do nothing to improve it!

So stop rebelling against your husband or wife or your boss, and begin to rebel against yourself. Perhaps you will object that if you don't rebel against other people they will go on ill-treating you. If you think that it just shows that you haven't understood the first thing about it! If you want them to change towards you, you must not fight them. If you change your own ways, your own attitude, they will sense it, and when they see that you have become luminous, radiant and intelligent they will be led to change themselves. In other words, it is by rebelling against yourself that you can overcome and transform others. This is the method I have found for myself. How can you possibly hope to overcome so many enemies in any other way?

Rebel against yourselves so as to free yourselves, for your real enemies are within. Don't look for them on the outside, they are inside you, and they are preparing some very unpleasant surprises for you. You will sometimes hear someone declare, 'Women! I'm finished with them. They've brought me nothing but problems and disappointment. Never again!' But as he has never done anything to combat the entities within, they are still there, still egging him on to repeat the same pattern of behaviour, so he is bound to suffer again in the same way. They are very wily, those entities within! They tell him, 'Poor fellow, it's true that all the women you've known so far have been cruel and fickle, but the one who has captivated your heart now is different: she'll bring you joy and inspiration.' And the poor fool believes them and tumbles into the trap once more!

How can I make you understand that the entities whose advice you follow may seem to be your friends, but this is only a camouflage? In reality they are your enemies, and their only ambition is to suck you dry and destroy you. And you, foolishly, you flatter and spoil and nourish them with your most precious energies. Well, the time has come for you to rise up in revolt, and the first step is to recognize that your most dangerous enemies are not outside, but inside you. And when you have finally vanquished your inner enemies you will have no trouble vanquishing your external enemies by your example, your attitude and words, your expressions and your emanations. Why is that human beings have still not discovered these methods? Knives, revolvers and bombs have never resolved problems. What has happened since men started using them: have things got any better? So, begin by rebelling against yourself. There will be plenty of time to fight others later on, but then you will fight with arms of nobility and the all-powerfulness of love.

Always remember that Heaven is watching you from on high and taking note of the way you use all that wealth you have been given: are you using it for purely selfish ends or for a divine purpose? This is the only thing that matters. If you asked yourself this question every day, in all honesty, you would be able to improve so many aspects of yourself! Of course, you will not be able to remedy everything all at once, but at least you can develop more lucidity and awareness. If you don't do this you will never escape from the law of Karma.

As long as you have still not taken your own life in hand and started to do what has to be done in order to synchronize your vibrations with the divine vibrations of the cosmos, you will continue to be subject to the blind forces of nature. Most human beings are stuck at this stage for they have never been shown how important it is to work on their own inner reality. But you must realize that if you oppose Cosmic Intelligence by a way of life which is in contradiction to Its scheme of things, you will simply crumble away until there is nothing left of you. You probably think that Cosmic Intelligence must be very cruel if It destroys all those who oppose It; but in point of fact, Cosmic Intelligence does not even pay attention to them and It has certainly never wished to destroy anybody. But if you, because of your own stupidity and ignorance, hurl yourself against the immense forces of the Cosmos, you will simply be broken and annihilated by their power. It stands to reason. If one solitary wretch tries to pit himself against an army he will be wiped out in no time at all. If an insect keeps on banging against a window-pane until it is stunned, do you say that it's the fault of the window? Man behaves exactly like an insect: he is always struggling against Divine Law and banging his head against all the splendours of the Cosmos: he just enjoys a scrap! But this is the direct route to destruction, and it is not God who will destroy him but his own stubbornness.

A disciple's first concern is to put himself in harmony with Cosmic Intelligence and in order to do so he begins by being very careful about how he spends his energies : you must make a note of that !

Some of the things I tell you have to be applied every day, and others only when the occasion arises. And this, that I have been telling you today, should be present in your minds every single day, for I shall not always be there to remind you. You can put a number of things to one side, but not this. You are expected to be conscious every single day, whatever the circumstances, of exactly how you are using your energies — especially as this is an exercise that can be done anywhere ! While you're walking to work, on the bus, in the dentist's chair or while you're preparing a meal in your kitchen — it is always possible for you to glance into yourself with the query, 'Now, let me see : if I do this, that or the other thing, what is it going to cost me ? Oh dear ! I can see that I'll end by being stripped of all that is pure and divine just to feed the pigs. No thank you, not for me ! I won't have anything to do with it ; my energies are not meant to be used to raise the dead.' As Jesus said, 'Let the dead bury their own dead, but you, the living, follow me.' As you can see : the question of how you use your energies is of vital importance for your evolution.

9

SACRIFICE,
THE TRANSMUTATION OF MATTER

I

Very few people are aware of the tremendous importance of adding something new and more powerful, something brighter and more luminous, to their lives every single day. They have no idea that the listless, sluggish life they are content to lead is actually very dangerous, because all kinds of physical and psychological diseases are just waiting for the right moment to worm their way in and start gnawing at them. Cosmic Intelligence did not intend man, who is so marvellously conceived and created, to spend his life half asleep and comatose. On the contrary, man is destined to make constant progress on the path of evolution until he reaches the level of the Angels — until he reaches God Himself.

In point of fact, man is not the only creature to be governed by the law of evolution. Every realm in creation, whether mineral, vegetable, animal or human, tends to evolve in the direction of that which is a step above its own.

Stones have been on earth longer than any other form of existence. They are inert, without feeling, without means of locomotion or growth. Their ideal, therefore, is to become plants.

The ideal of plants is to become animals. They are tied to the ground by their roots and can neither move nor feel things as animals can, and their ambition is to free themselves from the soil and move about. But there is one way in which their cells can evolve and that is by being assimilated into an animal's body: plants have no other way of evolving than by sacrificing themselves and allowing themselves to be eaten or burned.

The ideal of animals is to become human beings endowed with reason. The ideal of human beings is to become angels, and that of angels is to become archangels or divinities. On the ascending scale of evolution, each category of beings possesses qualities which the one below it does not have, and each one endeavours to reach beyond its own level, to approach the level of those above it.

But man can only rise to the level of the angels through fire, the fire of sacrifice. The etymology of the words can help us to understand this: the Latin for angel is *angelus,* for fire it is *ignis* and for lamb it is *agnus.* In Bulgarian, the word for angel is *anguel,* for fire it is *ogan* and for lamb it is *agné.* If one relates these words to

each other, one understands why Christ, the Son
of God, was compared to the lamb which had to
be sacrificed before the creation of the world.
Where does this tradition come from? In some
countries, in the past, when someone intended to
build a house, it was customary to sacrifice a
lamb as a holocaust, in order to ensure its protection and solidity. The intention was to remind
everybody that before the world could be created,
a 'lamb', that is to say a living being, had had to be
sacrificed so that the world would be built on a
firm, indestructible foundation. Christ is the
divine Lamb, the spirit of love, who has the power
to attract, support and bring things together; He
is the foundation stone of love on which creation
is built. It is He who sacrificed and immolated
Himself, thereby permeating the matter with
which this edifice is built. He is the bond, the
cement which holds the universe together.
Throughout the whole universe, from the pebbles
on the ground to the stars in the heavens, it is this
love which holds the whole framework together.
If love were to disappear, our bodies, too, would
begin to disappear, for it is the power of love
which holds all the cells and particles of our bodies together. Sacrifice represents the most exalted,
the most noble, the most divine manifestation of
love. Sacrifice is the Omega, the last letter, there is
no other. Jesus came in order to speak this last

letter. Others will come after him to apply it and bring it to completion, but they will not add anything greater than sacrifice: sacrifice remains, for all eternity, the most sublime act possible.

Sacrifice is the key to joy. Those who are capable of sacrifice are very privileged because they have understood the meaning of life, they are ready to be fathers and mothers. Everyone knows that fathers, mothers and children exist, but very few people are capable of understanding all that is contained in this simple image of a family. The existence of father, mother and child can teach us something very important. When someone is capable of sacrificing himself for others it means that he is mature and ready to become a father or mother. One who is incapable of sacrificing himself for others is still a child. On the physical plane he may have children of his own, but this is only an outward appearance and Heaven will not consider him a father or mother.

To be a father or mother is a very high ideal, but it is not ideal to remain a child. The true ideal is to become, first of all, a father or mother, and only then to become a child. Yes, because if you are already a fruit, you can then become a seed: this is your absolute right. But if you have not yet become a fruit, how can you possibly become a seed? You can't! Seeds can only come after the fruit, and in order to bear fruit you have to be a father or mother: you have to be capable of impersonal, disinterested love. The ideal, therefore, is to become a father or mother so as to be capable of bringing children into the world, and these 'children' are the sacrifices, the impersonal fruits of enlightened parents. Those who are incapable of sacrifice are incapable, also, of bringing children into the world because they are not yet mature.

A child reaches the stage of puberty when he is thirteen or fourteen. Puberty is a phase in the process by which a human being is transformed from an egotistical, personal being into a fully mature man or woman, capable of giving, of producing fruit, in other words, of making sacrifices. Before the age of puberty, a child is like a sterile soil which needs to receive and absorb everything for itself. But once he has reached puberty he becomes capable of producing fruit, on both the physical and the psychic levels. This is why I say that if you don't have that spring of clear water within you, that is, if your love is not pure and disinterested, you will shrivel and dry up; you will never produce a harvest; you will have neither flowers nor fruit; you will be a desert, a wilderness. And who wants to linger in a wilderness?

It goes without saying that the sacrifices you decide to make must be sensible ones. Some people decide to 'sacrifice themselves' by marrying a particular man or woman in the belief that they will be able to save them from drink or mental disease! But will they really be able to save them? The Lord only knows! You see, there is no lack of generosity and kindness here: what is lacking is the light. People are so blind they don't foresee what will happen. And it is such a waste to throw away all those qualities and virtues on something that is doomed to failure. It would be much better to dedicate them to a divine work that will help thousands of people, not just one. Especially as there is no guarantee that that one individual will, in fact, be helped. What is far more certain is that the person who has sacrificed himself in order to help him will be his own victim.

Make up your minds to dedicate all your efforts to a divine ideal, then the sacrifices you make for this ideal will be transformed into gold, light and love. This is the secret. The great secret lies in the idea, the ideal for which you are working. If you work for yourself, if you are only interested in satisfying your own ambitions, appetites and passions, then whatever sacrifices you may make in pursuit of your goal will simply turn into ashes, not into light. A great many people make tremendous sacrifices in terms of money and of their own health, but as their goal

is a worldly one their sacrifices are not very fruitful. This is what people fail to realize: the importance of the idea behind each and every one of
their undertakings. The idea is the magical
aspect, the Philosopher's Stone which turns every
undertaking to gold. This is why I keep telling you
to work for this divine ideal that light may triumph in the world, that the Kingdom of God be
established on earth. Everything you do for this
idea will turn to gold, that is, to health, beauty,
light and strength.

We must give our lives to the Lord, saying,
'From now on I shall give up all the passing
pleasures and enjoyments which do me no good,
and work for the Kingdom of God.' And gradually, more and more, you will sacrifice all the
activities which defile you, and all the base
impulses which make you give way to anger,
jealousy and hatred. Why? Because it is these vile
impulses and habits which keep your spiritual
forces captive and prevent you from producing
fruit, and by renouncing them you free those
forces within you. Take a lesson from a tree: when
it is infested with insects it cannot give fruit and
has to be treated with insecticides. In the same
way you must rid your body, heart and will of all
the senseless pleasures which, like so many para-
sites, are sucking you dry of all the sap which
should be going to nourish your higher Self. You

cannot produce fruit or make sacrifices because you are harbouring quantities of other beings which are soaking up all your energies. You must get all those insects and caterpillars out of your system.

I could give you a whole host of examples to help you understand this idea. Take a bottle, for instance: if it is already full, how can you put anything more into it? You cannot. You have to begin by emptying it. In the same way, if a human being does not empty himself of his vices and pernicious habits, how can he make room for the divine virtues and qualities that are waiting to get in? He can't, because he is already full up! So this is the reason for sacrifice: to empty oneself, to clear out one's bad habits so as to be able to fill oneself with something else. As soon as one sacrifices a weakness, a virtue jumps into the empty space!

The Book of Nature is always there, lying open before you, and it contains everything you need to guide you through life. Why can't you understand it? Why are your eyes unable to see and your ears unable to hear? Because you are too busy with all kinds of amusements and pleasures which get in your way. Once you make up your minds to sacrifice these amusements and pleasures you will discover the existence of some extraordinarily powerful forces, your eyes will be opened and you will find that you can read everything contained in the Book of Nature. This is the secret.

Sometimes you find yourself faced with something totally incomprehensible and you think, 'I simply don't understand. Why can't I understand? Other people seem to...' Well, now you are in a position to answer your own question: 'It is because I am still indulging myself in inferior pleasures and pastimes which rob me of my energies. That's why I have none left for my inner eye.' There is no need to look further for the explanation of why you cannot see. You simply have to divert your energies from those inferior activities and put them to work elsewhere so that they can arouse other cells which are still dormant. But people are very ignorant; they say, 'I must keep this one little pleasure. It would make me miserable to give up everything!' But how can they be so dense? Heaven has never asked us to give up all pleasure, only to seek pleasures of a higher order, to find purer, subtler pleasures. The more one gives up the transient, fleeting pleasures of life, the more one is flooded by true joy. He who is capable of understanding me today will completely change his whole life, for what I have given you is not just words, it is reality.

Transmutation of spirit into matter

II

Most people associate the word 'sacrifice' with the idea of difficulty, loss and suffering. Well, that is where they make a great mistake! Initiatic Science tells us that sacrifice is not a deprivation or loss but a substitution, a transference, a change of level. The same activity is involved, but on another level and with other, purer, more luminous materials.

Sacrifice, therefore, is the transformation of one kind of matter into another kind, of one kind of energy into another; one deprives oneself of something in order to have something better in its stead. That is sacrifice. Take a lump of coal: it is black, dirty and ugly; sacrifice it and it becomes fire, heat, light and beauty. He who refuses to make any sacrifices condemns himself to perpetual cold, ugliness and darkness.

Of course, as long as you still believe that sacrifice is going to deprive you and make you suffer, you will never be ready to sacrifice anything. So the sooner you adopt the initiatic point of view the better; it will teach you that when you renounce something it must always be in order to replace it by something better. Suppose you want to renounce a bad habit: gambling, for instance, or drink or women. If you don't put something else in its place it will keep coming back to tempt and torment you because you have not cultivated another need strong enough to overcome that old, ingrained vice. In fact, if all you do is repress your old habit, you may even be putting yourself in grave psychological danger. As long as human beings fail to understand this they will continue to inflict great suffering on themselves and then, naturally, they will come to the conclusion that it is not worth trying to make sacrifices because, not only is one bound to fail, but one only suffers all the more.

You must not deprive yourself of anything; you must not renounce anything; you must simply change your position and continue to do, on a higher level, what you did on the lower level. Instead of drinking foul water from an insanitary swamp you must drink the crystal-clear waters of a pure spring. If you don't drink at all you will die! So if you have been told not to drink, don't believe it; you must not drink sewage, true, but you must drink, so drink divine waters. This idea is expressed symbolically in Genesis: when Adam and Eve were in the Garden of Eden, God told them to eat the fruit of all the trees in the Garden except the fruit of the Tree of the Knowledge of Good and Evil. God never wanted to deprive Adam and Eve of food, He only wanted them to understand that some kinds of food are better and more nourishing than others.

A truly spiritual man does not deprive himself: he eats and drinks and breathes and loves, but in realms and on a level of consciousness unknown to ordinary men. When they hear talk of renunciation most people are terrified; they say, 'If I have to give up everything that makes life worth living, I'll die!' And they are right, of course, because if they don't realize that renunciation can give them something even better they will die! It is not a question of having to stop drinking, sleeping, breathing, loving and procreating, but of doing all these things better. You have to remember to effect this exchange every day so as to keep things in motion and create a flow of energies, otherwise stagnation and decay set in and all you have is mould and mildew. New waters have to flow through your life every day, and the only way to be sure of having a ready supply of new water is to keep in touch with Heaven by prayer and meditation every single day. For the genuinely new comes from Heaven alone.

Of course, men and women have often found out for themselves this solution of replacing things. When a woman has a husband who gives her nothing but problems, for instance, she tries to get rid of him and find another to take his place ! Human beings follow the precepts of Eternal Wisdom instinctively ; the only trouble is that these precepts are not always correctly applied. A man may think that if he changes wives he will be much better off, but there is no guarantee that he will find true happiness. It is quite possible that he will simply exchange one shrew for another, even worse ! Or a population may overthrow the political party in power but the next one will not necessarily be any better. Human beings feel, vaguely, that they have to change things but their mistake lies in thinking that they have to change things on the outside, whereas they should change things in themselves.

Now, let's get back to the example of fire that I mentioned a moment ago : why do you suppose that when an Initiate is about to perform a magic rite, or when a priest is going to say Mass, they light a candle so that light will be present at the ceremony ? What I am about to reveal to you in this connection is extremely important and when you understand it you will be obliged to put it into effect in your lives. In order to feed the flame, a candle has to provide it with the raw materials and, in doing so, the candle itself shrinks and diminishes. Combustion, therefore, is a sacrifice. If there were no sacrifice there would be no light. Light and fire both require nourishment in order to exist, and that nourishment is the candle. And each one of us represents a candle; we have all kinds of combustible materials in us, the black, lifeless materials of our faults and failings. The fire of sacrifice is the only thing that can bring them to life and make them shine and, for this to happen, there has to be a spark to set fire to them.

As long as man continues to live an ordinary, workaday life, he will be like the black, lifeless wood of a dead tree. He will shine and glow and be filled with life, beauty and warmth only when he has been visited by the fire of the spirit. But before this can come about he has to sacrifice his selfish life. It is the fear of disappearing altogether that prevents human beings from making this sacrifice. Of course, something has to disappear, that is true, but it has to disappear so that something else may appear. The wax of the candle disappears so that light and warmth may appear. You will say that, after a while, the candle will be consumed and disappear completely. That is true, but man can go on burning indefinitely. Once lit he cannot be put out : he will always have enough matter to fuel the fire.

The very best thing that could happen to anyone is to be set ablaze by the sacred fire of divine love, for it is only in that blaze that you will find the secret of life. The vast majority of human beings have not yet been set alight; they refuse to sacrifice any part of their lower nature; they refuse to be consumed by fire, so they remain stiff and cold like unlit candles. They must make up their minds: if they want that light and warmth to be theirs, one day they are going to have to decide to throw everything on to the fire. Look at a bonfire: what pleasure we get from throwing logs on it to feed the flames! All those dead branches could have gone to waste and been left to rot. But once they are ablaze, what delight they give us! And all the energies stored away in them are released and rush away, up to the sun from which they came. The crackling you hear as the wood burns is the sound of the rejoicing, the jubilation of all that energy freeing itself. It is the sound of chains bursting, of prisoners breaking free from their prison.

The reason for the custom of lighting a candle or burning incense when one prays is that the burning candle or incense is a symbol of sacrifice: certain results can be obtained only if one allows oneself to be consumed by fire. Nothing can be achieved without sacrifice. Sacrifice, which transforms energies by moving them onto a higher plane, is the only way to heal and enlighten human beings. Sacrifice is the veritable alchemical transmutation. Every time I light a fire or a candle I am struck by the profound significance of the phenomenon of sacrifice; it always reminds me that, for there to be light, even the inner light of intelligence, the light of the mind, sacrifice is necessary: we always have to burn something within us.

Human beings have so much clutter inside them that they could burn if they would! If only they would burn all their impurities, all the selfish, passionate impulses that drive them towards outer darkness, they would produce such brilliant light, such tremendous forces that they would be totally transformed. But instead of burning all that useless clutter, they cling to it for dear life! They are waiting until they are dying of cold (in other words, until they find themselves deprived of all love, friendship, tenderness and affection) as in those terrible periods of intense cold, when one has nothing left to burn but some old sticks of furniture. Yes, men have to experience terrible trials and tribulations and cruel disappointments before they finally decide to burn all the junk that has been accumulating inside them for centuries. But that day will come — and it will come for everybody! And for those who have understood

me, what a delight it is going to be to throw all
their mouldy, worm-eaten rubbish on to the fire.
What a blaze it will make!

It is our lower nature, our personality, which
is destined to feed our spirit. You must get this
into your heads once and for all and stop wondering why you have this troublesome lower nature
and how to get rid of it! You must not try to get
rid of it. Without it you could not survive on
earth, whereas with it you have all the elements
you need to nourish your spirit. You have to
understand that there is a law of magic by which,
if you wish to obtain results on a very high level,
you have to sacrifice something of your personality because, in doing so, you release the energies
needed to fuel a successful operation. This law is
the reason behind the ritual sacrifices which have
existed in all the religions of the world from the
beginning of time. When the men of old wanted
the gods to grant the success of some undertaking, they immolated animals as a sacrifice. The
idea was that the energies contained in the spilt
blood would be disseminated into the surround-
ing atmosphere and nourish certain entities who
would then collaborate in the success of the
undertaking. But then Jesus came, and he taught
men not to sacrifice external things any more:
animals, fruit, flour, oil and so on, for, even
though these things represented a real renuncia-

tion for those who offered them, it was still not as vital a sacrifice as to cure oneself of a weakness or give up something one covets and lusts after. It is this kind of renunciation which constitutes true sacrifice.

So Jesus came and he asked us to stop immolating the animals around us — the poor creatures have done nothing to merit such a cruel fate — and to immolate those inside us instead. And as it is our lower nature which gives shelter to all these beasts, it is this nature that has to be consumed by the fire of sacrifice so that all the forces it contains may be released. When this happens, the spirit, in the form of light, heat and life, is present in abundance.

Of course, there is already a form of combustion going on in the physical body and it is thanks to this combustion that life exists. But the fire in the physical body only provides energy for the purely vegetable, biological life. The life I am talking about is the spiritual life and the situation, here, is not the same : it is no longer the physical body which is burning, it is the lower Self, and although we cannot see it, it is immense, and it makes a huge bonfire ! You can expect to warm yourself and be lit by this fire for centuries to come !

At the moment, unfortunately, men are not yet burning their lower nature, they are only burning their physical bodies. Have you never noticed how people shrink and dwindle away as they get older? This physical combustion is natural and perfectly normal; there is no reason to worry about it. But the combustion of our lower nature is something we should think about every day of our lives so as to be sure of having enough light and heat for ever.

10

VAINGLORY AND DIVINE GLORY

There is a story about a disciple who went to see his Master and said to him, 'I'm not at all satisfied with the size of my body. I want to be as big as the sun so that I can fill the whole of space so that everyone in the whole world can see me! Please help me to fulfil my desire.' The Master granted his disciple's request and, lo and behold, the disciple became gigantic; everybody could see him from miles away and many scientists and philosophers arrived and started to study this phenomenon and invent all kinds of theories about where he came from. As for the disciple himself, he was delighted to be the object of such universal interest! Not long after that another disciple went to the same Master and said, 'My size makes it impossible for me to study everything as I would like to. I'm much too big. I want to become so small that I can slip in and out of even the tiniest nooks and crannies of nature.

Dear Master, please grant me my desire.' Here
again the Sage did as his disciple asked. But
before very long both disciples found themselves
in a terrible fix: they had not foreseen that they
would soon tire, one of being gigantic and the
other of being microscopic, and they had
neglected to ask their Master how they could
return to normal!

I don't know where that story comes from,
but one thing I do know, and that is that those two
disciples were very ignorant: they did not know
that the whole of life is based on a perpetual alter-
nation between expansion and contraction. Yes:
bigness and smallness are the two poles between
which life fluctuates, and the danger for man,
just as for the two disciples in this story, is to want
to remain stationary at one pole. Of course, the
tendency to grow bigger and bigger and take up
more and more room is universal; even babies
share it: from the moment they are born, they
keep getting bigger and heavier! Once he has
finished growing in his physical body, man wants
to grow in other ways, by acquiring more and
more money, material possessions or renown, for
instance, or by winning first place in competi-
tions and contests of various kinds. Artists, scientists and philosophers all want to take up as much
space as possible in their own field: art, science or
philosophy. And even those who dedicate their

lives to the Lord want to win first place amongst His servants. You probably remember reading in the Gospels about the mother of the Apostles James and John, who begged Jesus to give her two sons the privileged places at his right and left hand when he came into his Kingdom.

In itself, there is nothing reprehensible in wanting to be first. In fact God Himself has sown this desire in men's hearts. You will perhaps object that it is vanity, and you are right, of course. But isn't it vanity that has driven so many people to perform so many shining deeds? Of course, it is true that it is not they but others who benefit most from their deeds of glory: the vain man who does them is mainly interested in pleasing others and winning their approval and admiration. Performing artists, especially, have a great deal of vanity, but what tremendous pleasure and enjoyment they give us through their art, even though they, themselves, are often gloomy, unhappy people.

Vanity only becomes a problem if it is motivated by purely selfish considerations, if it drives someone to try to satisfy his desires at the expense of others, by ejecting or riding roughshod over all his rivals. But if one wants to be richer and more powerful than anyone else in order to help the poor, for instance, or to start an industry that would be to everyone's benefit then, of course, it is quite different.

As for the opposite tendency, the tendency to remain unknown and insignificant which we see in certain people with no ambition: is that reprehensible? It all depends. If you have opted for the spiritual life and are getting closer to the love and light of the Lord every day, and you remain tolerant, gentle and humble with others and refuse to use your superiority as a stick to beat them with, then, of course, it is wonderful. But if your modesty is simply due to a listless, narrow-minded outlook on life, then there is nothing wonderful about it. Your attitude benefits neither yourself nor anyone else! Both tendencies, therefore, can be either good or bad and both must be guided by wisdom and love.

Left to itself, without discipline and guidance, the ambition to achieve greatness can be harmful, if not to others, at least to the person concerned. History contains many examples of men and women who were so determined to surpass their fellow men by their science or their conception of life that, little by little, they became isolated and estranged from others and suffered a great deal from their solitude. They had the glory they coveted, of course, their name was on everyone's lips, but they were still alone, for they had forgotten that they were living on earth and that it was important to keep in touch with other human beings.

The truth is that one has to know how to fluctuate between the two extremes and be very big at some moments and very small at others. Let me give you an example. When a Magus, or even a simple priest, is about to perform a special ceremony he puts on sacerdotal robes and sumptuous, gemstudded vestments. But once the ceremony is over he dresses in ordinary clothes like everybody else. During the ceremony he manifests the power and glory of the spirit, and afterwards he reverts to his natural attitude of simplicity. And in fact, even if a Master does not put on ceremonial robes, he sometimes seems so immense and of such sublime grandeur to his disciples, that they are too dazzled and bemused even to recognize him. Then, if they meet him again a few hours later, they find that he is exactly as they have always known him, simple and accessible, as though nothing had happened. This proves that the Master is both wise and full of love. Full of love, because he does not want to distance himself from his fellow men for too long, and wise because a human being, even the greatest Initiate, cannot stay at such a sublime level; it would require too great a tension, the cost in psychic energy would be too high and his nervous system would be unable to stand up to the strain.

People who always look as though they were floating on a cloud of inspiration miles above the mere world, as though they were always in direct communication with Heaven, are simply acting a part: it is not possible to sustain this level of consciousness without interruption. But even if they are only playing a part, they are still overloading their nervous system, for there is nothing more exhausting than to force the muscles of the face to maintain an artificial expression which does not correspond to a genuine inner state of mind. Your face muscles need to relax; so you would do better not to try to play a part for which you are not cut out and be content to be perfectly simple and natural.

You have to know when to let people see how big you are, and when to let them see how small you are. As I have said, your heart, which expands and contracts alternately, can teach you this. And if your heart possesses this wisdom why can't you be as wise as your heart? Unfortunately this wisdom is in very short supply, particularly with women: they are always anxious to appear more expressive, more lovable, more inspired and more affectionate than they really are. This is especially true when a woman meets a friend whom she has not seen for a long time: she is so anxious to show her friend how happy and successful she is that she acts a part. And then, when her friend has left, she is so strung up that she bursts into tears on the slightest pretext. If someone asks, 'What's the matter?', she will say, 'Oh, it's nothing. Just nerves!' Of course it is nerves, and no wonder: she has been pushing herself too hard! But why live such an artificial life? Why try to pull the wool over everybody's eyes? It is a question of vanity, of course, and a very stupid kind of vanity it is, too!

So, you see, vanity makes things swell up and get bigger, whereas modesty restores them to their normal size. But vanity can drain all your resources. Picture someone who gives endless parties and receptions because he wants everybody to know how rich he is; when the money begins to run short, instead of reducing his expenses he will borrow more money and go on entertaining just as lavishly until, one day, he finds that he is completely ruined. And this example applies to so many people in so many different ways: all ruined by their vanity because they wanted others to think that they were exceptional beings! So, always keep this in mind: vanity exhausts and impoverishes one, whereas modesty and simplicity help one to recuperate one's energies. That is why wisdom advises us to retain our simplicity. Even if only for a few hours or a few days, be simple and retiring so as to recuperate the energies you have been obliged to spend in trying to help others, in trying to enlighten them and share some of your wealth with them.

Man has been created in order to have a part in divine glory. This idea is symbolized in the Gospels by the parables of a banquet. We read that, at one of the banquets, one of the guests was refused admittance because he was not wearing the proper festive raiment. This means that in order to be admitted to the banquets prepared for us in Heaven, we must put on beautiful, luxurious clothes and jewelry — symbolically speaking. Yes, but when the feast is over, you have to take off all those festive garments and retire into a discreet hiding place so as to be ready for the next party!

If you were observant you would have noticed that man's everyday life faithfully reproduces these alternating movements. In the morning he gets up, dresses and goes out to manifest himself in various ways. In the evening he goes home, retires to his bedroom and closes the door, undresses, gets into bed, puts out the light and goes to sleep. And the next day the whole process begins all over again. Man is always either appearing or disappearing; he knows these two laws instinctively. But then why does he never know when to apply them in other areas? Why does he never know when to advance and when to retreat? When to show himself and shine before others and when to fade out or — as they say in stage parlance — to retire into the wings? Since his periods of retirement or disappearance are simply periods of recuperation of his energies, if someone does not know how or when to retire he will never recuperate — like all those who spend their days and nights overworking and end by being drained and exhausted: at some point they do disappear, and often for good! But that is a forced disappearance and it is not a good idea at all!

II

Everyone possesses an inner force which continually urges him to improve, to advance, to better his situation; but he still does not know exactly what that force is because it assumes all kinds of different aspects. And yet, in point of fact, it is easy to recognize it: if it is turned towards the world, to the quest for worldly possessions and material success, if it seeks to glitter and impress, then we can be sure that it is vainglory and it is better not to cultivate it. But if it is turned towards Heaven, that is to say, if it shows itself as a desire to do God's will and to earn a place amongst His chosen ones, then it is not vainglory but 'divine glory', for it is a yearning to be in touch with eternity and it must be encouraged and given room to grow.

Let me illustrate this with a very simple example: the question of clothes. Some people are outraged by the way aristocrats dressed in the past : all those velvets and silks and satins, all that lace, and the pearls and precious stones ! What was the point of all that window-dressing ? Was it simply to attract attention and impress people ? Well, if you look at old paintings of Angels, Archangels and Divinities you will see that heavenly beings were never depicted in rough clothes, on the contrary, in all the countries of the world artists have always shown them clothed in sumptuous silks and brocades richly embroidered with gold and precious stones. And in this case, except for a few narrow-minded individuals who refuse to recognize the law of correspondences, nobody waxes indignant about it. That is because, unconsciously, we all feel that there must be a correspondence between outer riches and inner riches, between the beauty of the inner reality and that of the outer raiment.

Besides, you know that on the invisible level a Saint, Prophet or great Master is always dressed in sumptuous garments adorned with precious stones, and these garments are the aura. The true raiment of an Initiate is his aura, with all its varied colours and precious stones which represent his qualities and virtues. You have certainly read the Bible story of Joseph, whose father, Jacob, gave him a tunic of many colours which aroused the envy of Joseph's brothers. Joseph's many-coloured coat was, of course, the symbol of his aura. Then, too, remember the priestly vestments worn by the High Priest of Israel: the ephod and, especially, the pectoral with its twelve precious stones.

This tradition of sacerdotal vestments and jewels has been preserved throughout the ages, even to our own day, and always with the same meaning: the richness of the outward raiment is an expression of the inner richness of the wearer. But they have another function also, a magical function: not only do they influence the celebrant who wears them, raising him to a more sacred, more mystical state, they also influence the spirits of the Invisible World whom he wishes to attract or repel. Obviously, though, what is essential is what takes place in the heart and soul of the priest or Initiate, for however glorious the vestments he wears, it is not in their power to confer gifts of greatness, purity, wisdom and power on him if he does not already possess them.

It is evident that there is no longer a close correspondence between the inner and outward appearance of human beings today: one sees people who are outwardly poor and ugly but inwardly rich and very beautiful, and vice versa. I have already explained the reason for this. But in Heaven, in the divine world, the correspondence between the inner and outer realities is always absolute. You will perhaps be surprised by this and ask, 'But is there such a thing as an outward appearance in the Invisible World?' Yes, of course there is: for every virtue, quality or force there is a corresponding form, medium or vehicle. We always talk of the entities above as spirits, but they are not pure spirits. Every spirit, however exalted, has a body, but it is made of such subtle, transparent, crystalline material that it is invisible to our eyes. Spirits have bodies which correspond exactly to the forces and qualities they possess, just as necklaces, coronets and other jewelry correspond to spiritual acquisitions, since pearls and precious stones are the symbols of specific virtues. But nowadays, of course, you will see people wearing magnificent clothes and jewelry that they do not deserve. It is all a sham! They try to draw attention to their outward splendour in order to conceal their inner poverty.

And yet there is nothing basically wrong with the desire to show oneself in the best possible light. In fact you could say that it is Nature herself who has planted this tendency in the heart of man in order to oblige him to evolve. It often happens that, thanks to their desire to win the approval and admiration of others, people are led to surpass themselves. Men have conquered their fears, for instance, and won acclaim as heroes simply because they did not want to let their family or their country down. An actor or a concert pianist, for example, is continually perfecting his art so that his public shall never tire of him or his work. And parents, teachers and educators make use of this tendency in children in order to stimulate them to work better. When you show a child that you trust him to work well, that you expect great things from him, he will do his best to live up to your expectations. You can even help a delinquent child to work well if you give him a responsibility and make him feel that you really trust him. For my part, at least, this is the method I use with young people: I always show them what they could become, the glorious life that could be theirs if they worked in accordance with the divine rules, and I have seen how this idea can really transform them.

Vanity, therefore, is an excellent tendency as long as you use it to further your evolution. I have never denied that I am very vain, but the thing is that I'm not interested in the applause of men: the Lord alone knows how one is obliged to twist and contort oneself to satisfy human beings. No, the only thing that interests me is to win the approval of the sublime Entities on high, and it is this ambition that obliges me to develop all that is best and most beautiful in myself. And then there is one aspect which is important, and that is that vanity always has some relationship to beauty. When someone is beautiful he has the spontaneous desire to let others see and admire him, whereas someone who has no hope of being admired is not particularly keen to show himself to others. A woman who has just stained her dress or torn her stockings is not going to make an exhibition of herself by dallying in the most brightly lit streets; on the contrary, she will hurry home, keeping to the shadows as much as possible.

It was Nature, therefore, which endowed man with vanity and, one must admit, it is a more natural thing than pride. Pride is not natural; in fact there is something monstrous about it. So, don't try to get rid of your vanity, otherwise you will never do anything worthwhile. Ah, my precious vanity: I would be completely lost without it! So I take great care of it, but I also take great care that it should serve me and not the other way round, otherwise I know very well where it would lead to. I understood, a very long time ago, that vanity can be very useful, that one can make it work for one, on one condition: that one realize just how dangerous it is to want to be glorious for oneself. What is important is to glorify the Lord, to glorify the sublime ideal for which one is working. If you always remember this, one day you will bathe in the glow of divine glory. So, you too must learn to direct your vanity towards the best possible target, towards the highest goal.

You could say that there are two kinds of vanity: an inferior and a superior kind. The inferior kind of vanity drives one to expand on a horizontal plane and the superior kind drives one to grow upwards, to expand vertically. The great drawback to the inferior kind of vanity is that it immediately arouses the jealousy and hostility of others because it shows off and blows its own trumpet to draw attention to itself. If your name is everywhere: on posters for films and plays, on the labels of dozens of household products, on the advertising pages of all the leading magazines, it is inevitable that some people will feel your success as a personal affront. They too had ambitions, they too dreamed of success and fame, but it is you who have triumphed and they resent it bitterly. Whereas if you leave them to their shady deals and concentrate on perfecting yourself spiritually, on becoming more and more attuned to the Lord, then, believe me, you will not find nearly so many people getting in your way and competing with you!

11

PRIDE AND HUMILITY

Vanity likes nothing better than to show everybody how kind, friendly and generous it is. It goes out and about in order to be seen, it engages in good works in order to draw attention to itself, it makes itself useful in order to be appreciated. But one thing is certain: although some may benefit from it, it is often very detrimental to the person who manifests it. As for pride, it is of no use to anybody, even others. The proud man is harsh and scornful of others; he too wants to be appreciated and respected but without lifting a finger to do anything for others. He is so convinced of his own merits that he never goes out looking for approval: he expects others to seek him out and discover his exceptional merits for themselves. He is like a mountain peak, alone and ice-bound. Others have to climb up to get to him and even then he is often remote and inaccessible. And when the proud man realizes that others neither respect nor admire him, that his superiority is not generally acknowledged, then he shuts himself up in his own darkness. In the vain man there is at least some light — a rather smoky light, it's true, but at least he makes an attempt to shine. But the proud man is dark and sombre, he comes under the reign of Saturn whereas the vain man is more influenced by Jupiter.

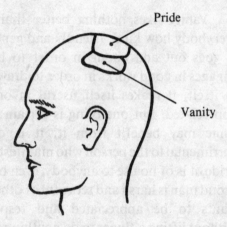

Figure 5 – The centres of pride and vanity
on the human skull

If we look at what phrenology has to tell us about this we shall see that the centre of vanity is slightly to one side of the skull, whereas the centre of pride lies on the median axis, slightly to the rear. But pride and vanity are not peculiar to man; they can be seen, too, in the animal and vegetable kingdoms. In the animal kingdom, a hen, for instance, is vain whereas a cock is proud; a horse is vain but a donkey is proud. And if you look at the vegetable kingdom, you can see that sweet melons are vain but water-melons are proud, tomatoes are vain and leeks proud. On the level of human beings, one can say that, generally speaking, women are vain and men are proud. A proud woman is a man in disguise and a vain man is a woman in disguise. Vanity seems to suit a woman better than pride. But there is both pride and vanity within each one of us, for the intellect is inclined to pride and the heart to vanity. As the intellect develops it becomes proud and cuts itself off from others while the heart, on the other hand, being inclined to vanity, feels the need to show off its possessions and abilities to others.

You could say that the Initiates of Antiquity were characterized by pride: they kept a jealous guard on all their secrets and refused to reveal them to the masses. Nowadays, by contrast, Initiates tend to reveal their knowledge and give away their secrets; anyone who wants to can now have access to the secrets of Initiatic Science, so we can say that contemporary Initiates tend to be vain. And we can also say, if you like, that I am vain, too. Yes, and it is thanks to my vanity that you learn so much when you come here: if I were proud things would be very different !

But, for the moment, I would like to talk to you about pride, which is certainly the most difficult of all defects to overcome, even for Initiates and Masters. Many mountain climbers, who have often spent a good deal of time at great heights, know that when they are at the top of a mountain many of their failings and baser desires seem to fade, leaving them with a broader outlook and greater disinterestedness and generosity. But one thing never leaves them, and that is their pride. Just like trees which cannot survive above a certain altitude, our baser tendencies cannot survive beyond a certain spiritual height, but pride is the exception: like lichen which clings to even the highest summits, pride accompanies saints and Initiates all the way to the highest degree of evolution.

It is easy to get rid of other failings, but it is extremely difficult to get rid of pride, especially as it is capable of disguising itself and passing itself off as all kinds of good qualities and virtues, even the most noble. So many men and women have fallen by the wayside through pride: pride in their knowledge, their power or their sanctity ! In spite of great wisdom and purity, they failed to realize that their hearts had become hard — in fact some of them ended by believing that they were God Himself come down to earth. So, you see, it is extremely important for disciples to take precautions and defend themselves against pride from the very beginning.

What exactly is pride? It is simply a particular way of holding your head and looking at things. Oh, you can be sure that you won't find a definition like that in any dictionary. But don't I have the right to make some definitions of my own? And humility is also a position of the head. Don't worry: you will soon understand. Suppose, for instance, that you were in the habit of hanging your head and looking down at the ground. What would you see? Mice, beetles, ants and worms, by which I mean stupid, unreasonable, vicious people. Naturally, if you compare yourself to them you will think that you are extraordinarily intelligent and reasonable: a paragon of virtue! And you will begin to despise others and want to humiliate them. And there you are, that is pride: the comparison between yourself and those who are inferior to you. And humility is the exact opposite: it consists in holding your head up and looking up towards those who are better and more perfect — and when you compare yourself to such as these you find that you are not so wonderful as all that.

Initiatic tradition recounts that Lucifer was the greatest and the most beautiful of all the Archangels. His power was such that he began to think that he was God's equal and to want to dethrone Him. And that, too, is pride: to think that one is the equal of someone more perfect than oneself and to want to take his place. Seeing this, another Archangel rose and cried out: 'Who is like God?' which, in Hebrew is *Mi* (who), *Kha* (like), *El* (God), and the story adds that God, who was watching all this, spoke to that other Archangel, saying, 'From now on you shall be called Mikhael and you shall be Prince of the Heavenly Hosts.' If pride could cause the most powerful of all the Archangels to fall and drag others down with him, it stands to reason that it can do the same for ordinary human beings.

If we want to escape the clutches of pride we must make every effort to know our two natures, the higher and the lower Self, the individuality and the personality, about which I have so often spoken; we must know them intimately and learn to work with them. This is the only way to defend oneself and avoid being vanquished and enslaved by pride. And just as one can learn to subject vanity, anger and sexual energy to one's own will, pride, too, can be vanquished and put to work. Personally, I don't consider myself safe from the danger of pride if I don't do this work too.

Mankind has borne this burden of pride for millions of years; it has a good reason for existing and if we learn to dominate and control it and put it to work for us, then we can escape its hold on us.

The first indispensable condition for mastering our pride is to be able to recognize it in all its manifestations. A great many people mistake pride for humility and vice versa. When they see someone cringing and grovelling in front of the rich and powerful because he feels his poverty, ignorance and helplessness in comparison, they say that he's humble. And then, when they see someone who has the audacity to want to establish the Kingdom of God, they say, 'What pride!' But they are wrong in both instances! The former is not humble at all; he grovels before the rich and powerful out of weakness or necessity; he is incapable of behaving any other way. But just give him a smattering of wealth and power and you will see if he is humble!

You must beware of taking people at face value. You may think that someone looks so gentle that they wouldn't hurt a fly. Well, they may well look perfectly inoffensive and docile, but gentle and docile towards whom? Most people, once they have the means to impose their will on others, chuckle to themselves in secret and think, 'Aha, that so-and-so did me an injury in the past,

now he's going to get a good lesson!' and then
they hasten to revenge themselves. If, in spite of
the sudden acquisition of money and influence, a
man remains understanding and approachable,
you can be sure that his humility is genuine. But
until he has been put to the test you can never
be sure.

Look at how some supposedly humble people behave in the face of tribulation: so many
rebel against God — or even deny His very existence — as soon as they have some little difficulty
to overcome! True humility is not a question of
submitting to the rich and powerful of this world
or to tyrants; it is a question of submitting to the
divine world, to the Lord. To be humble is to have
an attitude of deep respect for all that is sacred, to
safeguard and defend it both in and around oneself. A great many people believe themselves to be
humble although they spend their time trampling
on divine precepts. No, no! Humility is an attitude of unconditional service, absolute availabil-
ity and absolute obedience to the Creator.

Some people think that Jesus was proud
because he declared himself to be the Son of God,
drove the merchants out of the Temple with a
whip and called the Pharisees 'brood of vipers',
'children of Satan' and 'white-washed tombs'!
But in fact he was not proud, because he submit-

ted to the decrees of Heaven and in the midst of the most terrible suffering he said, 'Father, not my will but Yours be done.'

A proud man is one who imagines that he is the only one that counts, that he is dependent on nothing and nobody. He is like a light bulb which flatters itself it can give light without in the least suspecting that if the current were switched off at the mains it would remain in darkness. A proud person believes that he is the source and origin of the various phenomena which take place in and through him, and this is why an Initiate, if he wants to avoid the lure of pride when he has gained a spiritual victory, must learn to say, not 'I have triumphed!' but, 'Lord, it is You who have triumphed through me. May all power and glory be Yours!'

A humble man is one who knows he is not alone. He knows that he can do nothing by himself and that if he did not cling to the Lord he would have neither strength, nor light nor wisdom. He senses that he is a link in an endless chain, a conductor of cosmic energy coming from infinitely far away and flowing through him to others. A humble man is a valley watered by the streams and rivers which flow from the mountain tops to fertilize the plains; he opens himself to the coming of these impetuous forces from the heights and his reward is a rich fruitfulness. The proud man, believing that he can depend on himself and forgetting where the active forces within him come from, ends, sooner or later, by losing everything he ever had. Men are very far from suspecting what tremendous wealth is inherent in humility.

Pride is a shortcoming of the intellect, and if you want to witness some of the most dazzling displays of pride in this world, go and listen to scientists, philosophers, artists and politicians proclaiming their ideas, their point of view, their 'creeds'. Every one of them thinks that he is the only one to possess the truth, the only one to reason correctly, and they are all ready to massacre others in order to impose their own convictions. As everyone knows, history is full of people who were so totally convinced that they possessed 'truth' and, even, that they were the avenging arm of God, that they laid waste whole cities and massacred hundreds of people in the name of their beliefs. Just look at what the Church did during the Inquisition! All those priests and bishops who thought they were so far above the masses that they had the right to exterminate those whom they judged to be in error! What pride, what presumption!

Just as long as people go on thinking that their own point of view is superior to all others, and go on pronouncing categorical judgments about everything, they will go on making mistakes, for this behaviour is in direct contradiction to a truly intelligent attitude. The truly intelligent attitude is humility; that is to say that true intelligence recognizes the existence of other beings above us who are superior to us and who have a much clearer, purer and more divine understanding of things. Only an idiot believes that his understanding of things is the ultimate, the *nec plus ultra*. An intelligent man says, 'Well, at the moment I think thus and so; I feel that this or the other is so; I understand things this way. But this doesn't mean that there are not other, more highly evolved beings in creation who could teach me a great deal and help me to understand better. I shall go and seek them out.' That is true intelligence.

But where will you find someone capable of reasoning so wisely? How many, instead, are ready to spill their blood (or, preferably, that of others) to prove that it is they who possess the truth! Unfortunately nothing engenders greater friction between human beings than conflicting ideas. Everybody is ready to tolerate moral weaknesses and failings in their friends and neighbours, but as soon as their political, philosophical or religious ideas are different or opposed, it is open war! You only have to look at the lessons history can teach us: how many very saintly people with exceptional gifts have been misunderstood and despised simply because their point of view was different! They were hanged or beheaded like common criminals, with no regard for their wisdom or moral worth. It is pride which blinds men to the merits of those whose ideas they contest. It is pride which pits men against each other and it is humility which restores peace and harmony.

Wisdom and intelligence, true, divine intelligence, are possessed only by those who are genuinely humble, those who know that they cannot put blind trust in the lucubrations of their own intellect. As long as the intellect, the lower mental faculty, talks, argues, makes a lot of noise and takes up all the available space, the higher mental faculty cannot get a word in. The higher mental faculty is the only one which enables man to see and understand the divine plan which he has been sent to earth to accomplish, and not only to see and understand, but also to carry it out. If man does not have the humility which alone enables him to go beyond the purely intellectual dimension, he will always miss the point. Only when he has succeeded in pricking the balloon of the intellect's swollen ego will his higher mental faculty be free to manifest itself and reveal to his wondering gaze the real marvels of the universe.

All those who are firmly convinced of the absolute truth of their opinions are proud. Perhaps you will ask, 'But then, does this mean that we should never think that we know the truth?' Certainly not, and I shall explain how you can avoid giving in to pride when you are convinced of the truth of your opinions. But, first of all, you must have a clear idea of the nature of intelligence and of the origin of your point of view and the opinions you hold.

Our intelligence is nothing more nor less than the sum total, the synthesis of the innumerable centres and organs in our bodies, of all the tendencies and innate urges that have accompanied us in one incarnation after another, for millions of years. It is a summary, an abstract of all the capacities and faculties possessed by all the cells that go to make up our organism. The quality of our intelligence is in direct proportion to the sensitivity, harmony and degree of evolution of our cells. It is extremely important to understand that intelligence is not a separate, distinct faculty with an independent life of its own; it is part of the whole man, including his cells and physical organs. And it is for this reason that to think correctly is not only the result of an effort of the intellect, it is the outcome of a whole way of life.

Now, let's take this a step further: where does our intelligence come from? It is a reflection of Cosmic Intelligence. But it is an imperfect reflection because, in the course of its passage through our physical cells which are often in a state of chaos caused by our passions, the light of Cosmic Intelligence is distorted and loses much of its brilliance. Cosmic Intelligence cannot manifest Itself perfectly through a creature who has not yet managed to control his own instinctive urges; but the more he purifies and perfects himself, the more capable he becomes of receiving and manifesting the light of that Intelligence.

Since a disciple's intelligence is a direct consequence of the condition of the cells of his body, he should be particularly careful to keep them as healthy and harmonious as possible by paying attention to the quality of his physical food, but also and primarily, to the quality of his psychic food (sensations, feelings and thoughts), otherwise he will remain closed to all revelations of a higher order. The only way to improve the quality of one's intelligence is to improve the quality of one's way of life. I have always believed this; I have always known it to be true, and I have always worked in this direction.

It is simply astounding to see how people lay down the law about something they know nothing about in the firm conviction that things are exactly what they say they are. They are even ready to exterminate others and destroy themselves for the sake of their convictions! They never stop to question their own authority: 'What if I were wrong, after all? Perhaps I'm not so highly evolved, so pure and receptive. Do I have the right to be so firmly convinced? I'd better try and find out; I'd better study things a little more closely.' Oh, no! They are ready to massacre others and to lay down their own lives, but they will never give up their own opinions.

But how can people be so convinced that they know all there is to know about everything: current events, religion, politics, love... everything you can think of? They often change their opinion about something radically in the space of only a few years, and yet, each time, they are just as convinced that they are right. In their youth they thought one thing, when they grew up they thought another and when they are old they think quite differently again. So why are they so attached to their ideas? Surely they should say to themselves, 'I've changed my opinion about this or that so many times, how can I be sure that what I think today is true?' Yes, even when you are ninety-nine you should say to yourself, 'I'm not ready to make my final judgment on that. Perhaps in a few thousand years I'll see things more clearly. I've already changed my opinion so many times in the course of my existence!' You have to be convinced, that's true. But not of the value of your own judgment, for it is very limited and liable to error. Live a little longer and you will see: you will change your opinion again several times!

Now that you understand to what extent we are all in danger of succumbing to the temptation of pride, take steps to safeguard yourselves. Remember, every day, to lift your head and look up and compare yourselves with those who are so far above you, the Angels, Archangels and Divinities, and you will realize that you are not really so remarkable after all! Instead of laying down the law about everything and proclaiming your own opinion as though it should be the criterion for every reasonable being, try to find out what Initiatic Science and the great Masters of humanity think about things, ask them to enlighten your mind so that you can model your opinion on theirs. All men necessarily have a distorted vision of things until they have compared their opinions and their point of view with those of Cosmic Intelligence. History shows this up very clearly, for after a few years it is easy to recognize the blunders committed by people who were too sure of their own opinions.

So there you have the very best method for resisting the wiles of pride. You know that, owing to mistakes you have made in past incarnations, your intelligence is very limited and that it would be catastrophic to rely on it, so you must get into the habit of consulting the divine world. Never let a day go by without looking up and saying, 'My opinion about such-and-such a thing, or such-and-such a person is thus and so. Am I right? Give me the light I need.' If you do this, not only will you be protecting yourself against pride but you will receive clear, truthful answers to all your questions and you can be sure of being on the right track. Never let yourself believe that you have reached perfection. No, you are only on the road to perfection: you have not arrived yet! Be very careful, for you can still make mistakes as long as you have not reached the summit.

But there is one thing I must add, and that is that those who are not really working seriously to change their way of life, those who continue to flirt with their baser appetites, even if they do ask for light and guidance from Heaven, will receive only misleading answers. They may think that what they receive is a true intuition but it will, in fact, be a false impression. And the reason for this is quite simple: as the message travels from Heaven it is obliged to pass through the layers of impurities accumulated within them, and by the time it reaches their consciousness it is necessarily distorted. The phenomenon is similar to the

optical illusion produced when you put a stick
half into water : it looks as though it were broken.
Yes, even advice from Heaven can be distorted if it
has to travel through layers of impurities. In fact
the risk of misunderstanding is so great that it
would be safer not to listen to what you hear. A
great many people have a certain capacity for
clairvoyance or mediumship and it is perfectly
true that they receive messages from the Invisible
World, but they would be well advised not to rely
on what they see or hear, because the message is
not pure, too many different elements have
become mixed up in it. Only those who make the
effort to purify and elevate themselves and to
shed their encumbrances can receive answers that
are true and clearly intelligible.

12

THE SUBLIMATION OF SEXUAL ENERGY

I

The story in the Book of Genesis of how the first man and woman, Adam and Eve, lived in the Garden of Eden and how they came to be expelled from the Garden, is an inexhaustible source of very meaningful symbols.

God had put the entire Garden of Eden at the disposal of Adam and Eve; the only thing He forbade them to do was to taste the fruit of the Tree of the Knowledge of Good and Evil. Why?

Paradise was a kind of alchemist's laboratory and our first parents were the alchemists whose task was to study the properties of all the elements symbolized by the trees growing there. If God forbade them to eat the fruit of the Tree of the Knowledge of Good and Evil it was because it contained elements which they were not yet strong enough to 'digest': they should have waited.

But Eve, whose curiosity was greater than Adam's, was fascinated by the tree and, although she did not dare to pluck any fruit, she could not take her eyes off it. Then, one very hot day, all of a sudden the serpent at the base of her spine woke up (for snakes wake up and become extremely agile in hot weather). So, as I say, it was very hot in Paradise that day — of course, all this is symbolic — and the serpent that had been asleep in Eve's spinal cord* woke up and whispered in her ear, 'Why don't you try it? Just taste it! What are you afraid of? If you eat that fruit you will become like God and that's why He has told you not to eat it.' Now, it was quite true that because of that fruit Eve would become like God, but only after millions and billions of years of suffering and distress in the course of innumerable reincarnations. So Eve ate the forbidden fruit and gave some to Adam. But they could not 'digest' it. God had told them that if they ate that fruit they would die, and they did die; they died to a certain level of consciousness. Before that day they had been free, happy, luminous and unrestricted by physical weight, and they died to this higher mode of

---

* See *Man's Subtle Bodies and Centres: the Aura, the Solar Plexus, the Chakras* (Collection Izvor No. 219), Chapter Six, in which the parallel is drawn between the Tree of the Knowledge of Good and Evil and the Chakra system and between the Serpent and the Kundalini force.

existence; they died to the light and joys of Heaven and came alive to the sufferings of earth.

The Snake in the Bible story, therefore, is a symbol, the symbol of man's sexual energy which he awoke but which he was unable to dominate. The snake wakes up when it is hot and goes to sleep when it is cold. Heat is a characteristic of all the passions; heat which consumes and destroys man's inner treasures. On this earth, the greatest concentration of wild animals and beasts of prey is to be found in equatorial forests where it is extremely hot, and someone who often ventures into his own equatorial zone (the stomach and sex) will meet the wild beasts of passion which will begin to proliferate and multiply within him.

The Serpent is often seen as the expression of evil in man although, in point of fact, this symbol is not entirely negative. On the contrary, the serpent is also seen as a symbol of wisdom, and this is particularly apparent in the Caduceus of Hermes.

To an Initiate, one of the serpents of the Caduceus is the symbol of sexual energy, the cause of evil, and the other is the symbol of the transformation of that energy into a new, extremely powerful force, the force of wisdom and clairvoyance. This is why the ancient Pharaohs of Egypt were often represented with a tiny serpent emerging from between their eyes: it was a sign that they had transmuted their sexual force by bringing it up to the level of the brain. And this transmuted force gives Initiates the power to see the subtle realities of the regions beyond our world. In some of the religions of Antiquity, in fact, serpents were an object of worship and were used as oracles and of course you have all heard of the Oracle of Delphi where the Pythia was believed to pronounce her oracles under the inspiration of the Python.

A sage who knows the laws and knows how to transform this power that lies dormant in every man, becomes a 'serpent', that is to say a wise and reasonable being. Indian sages are known as *nagi,* or 'snakes', expressing the idea that the forces of evil can be used for good if man knows how to transform them. In each one of us there is a snake coiled at the base of the spinal cord. This is the sleeping-place of Kundalini, that powerful force which can be used to perform miracles by Initiates who know how to arouse and master it. *

In the past, a great many religious people thought that sexual energy was a diabolical force which had to be thwarted at all costs! And what was the result? Well, the result was that they had no more life or vigour in them, their springs dried

* See *Man's Subtle Bodies and Centres* (Collection Izvor No. 219), Chapter Five 'Kundalini Force'.

up and they could no longer be moved by enthusiasm or joy. They imagined that that was the way to become saints. But that is not sanctity! Generations and generations of believers followed that path and what good has it ever done?

Obviously, there have always been a few, here and there amongst all those mystics, who had genuine gifts and exceptional intelligence and willpower which enabled them to surmount that terrible aridity. But even they never really fulfilled themselves because they did not know that man's sexual energy was a divine force given to him for his happiness and fulfilment and not, as they imagined, for his downfall!

Sexual energy is a very powerful force and it must be tapped in moderate amounts: it is a raw sap which has to be processed and transformed in the cells of the body and then diffused by the spirit throughout the whole organism, in the form of vitality on the physical plane, love and joy in the heart, light and wisdom in the brain. The power of sexual energy is tremendous, and the wise know how to control and channel it. They don't let it torment them or force them into tragic situations. They don't let it roar through their inner towns and villages like a tidal wave, destroying all in its path: they build dams, watermills, factories and irrigation canals, and then they can enjoy the harvest produced by all that power so wisely distributed. The more one resorts to reason in dealing with sexual energy, the more one amasses spiritual treasure. When sexual energy is mastered and under control it is exactly like the strong-flowing waters of a mighty river which have been channelled into dikes and ditches to irrigate the whole land, just as the Egyptians used the waters of the Nile to irrigate and bring prosperity to their country. The more man makes use of wisdom in drawing on his sexual energies, the closer he comes to the Kingdom of God and the clearer is his understanding of the meaning and of the beauty of life.

Sometimes one gets the impression that the more one explains the question of love from the initiatic point of view, the less human beings understand it. Why is this? It is simply because for thousands and thousands of years they have been endlessly repeating the same patterns of behaviour, the same practices. They seem unable to imagine that Nature could have planned that one sort of human sexual behaviour would be valid for a certain period of time, but that she should then wish to lead them away from those earlier patterns to the discovery of other, more elevated, more spiritual and far more beautiful manifestations. When one talks to them about this higher conception of love, they reply that if they are no longer allowed to satisfy their sexual needs they will die, because that is what makes them live! Yes, of course. That is what makes the roots live, but the flowers at the top of the tree are dying! So, it all depends on the person and his degree of evolution.

Human beings have been designed to evolve in all possible ways, so why should they not evolve in this area, the area of love? And this nobler conception, this more highly evolved manifestation of love consists in sublimating sexual energy and channelling it up to one's head, to feed the brain and give it the power it needs to produce its own marvellous creations. Love is a divine force which comes to us from on high, and we should, therefore, respect and cherish it and even do what we can to direct it back towards Heaven, instead of wasting it and letting it drain away into the sewers of Hell where it is sucked up and used by larvae, monsters and elementals. As long as men don't know about all the ways in which this force could be used for gigantic spiritual achievements they will continue to waste it, and this is why they are more and more indigent, and more and more like animals. Everyone knows that sexual energy tends to go in one direction, but very few even know that it is possible to channel it in another direction, or are interested in trying to do so.

Most people experience sexual energy as a terrible tension which they feel they must relieve. So they get rid of it without realizing that, in doing so, they are losing something very precious, a quintessence which they burn up mindlessly, simply for the pleasure they get out of it, whereas they could have used it to achieve a veritable regeneration of their whole being. Think of man as a skyscraper, fifty or a hundred storeys high, and that will help you to understand that that tension is necessary, because a lot of pressure is needed to pump enough water all the way to the top floor to supply those who live up there, so that they can wash, drink, water their flowers, etc. Without that tension the water would never get all the way up to the top. If human beings realized what this tension really was and if they knew how to set about it, they could use it to provide food and drink for their brain cells, for it is an energy which can be pumped all the way up to the brain through the channels which intelligent nature has designed especially for this purpose.

One might compare this system of canals and ducts to those in a tree. The mineral substances drawn from the soil by the root hairs make up the raw sap which is sucked up through the hollow fibres in the trunk until it reaches the leaves, where it is transformed into food for the flowers and fruit. A tree knows the alchemist's secrets for the transmutation of matter. And if a tree can know such secrets, why shouldn't man know them too?

So tension is useful and one should not try to get rid of it, for it can be used to pump energy all the way to the top. If the brain cells are not nourished by this energy, instead of being activated and used for gigantic achievements, they will remain numb, impoverished and chloroformed, just sufficiently alive to ensure that the lower, animal functions of the body continue, and that is all! As long as one has not learned to control oneself, one is depriving oneself of every chance of becoming strong, powerful and intelligent.

How can men and women be made to understand that Cosmic Intelligence intended these energies to be used for sublime creations? There seems to be no way! All they are interested in is their pleasure, anything that is easy, anything that requires no effort. Ah, yes! But that pleasure is going to have to be paid for and, in the long run, it will cost them a great deal. What they fail to realize is that if you make the effort to dominate and control yourself you not only become richer but you also experience extraordinary pleasure. But perhaps the word 'pleasure' is not really suitable in this context; it is always associated with the instinctive, lower manifestations: I should say 'joy', 'rapture' or 'ecstasy'. Pleasure is not something very noble or glorious, in fact one is often ashamed of it, whereas joy, rapture and ecstasy can only be experienced when the divine dimension in us stirs and begins to be active.

I want to say these things particularly to young people, for young people do not always realize that there are other experiences to be had which are far more enriching than those which interest them at the moment, and that if they go on as they are now, they will soon lose all their freshness and charm, all their beauty and light. Young people want to experience physical love? All right! But they will not find happiness simply by having one experience after another. After a while they will have forgotten all their pleasurable experiences and be left with the wreckage: regrets and increasing gloom. They must try to make an effort to control themselves. Even if they don't succeed at once, little by little they will get results and then they can take pride in having overcome and they will feel much stronger.

Perhaps some will ask what they can do to practise and become stronger. It is not difficult, there are hundreds of occasions when young people get together: on the street, at work, at parties or dances, on a trip, on the beach, etc. It is normal that, in certain circumstances, you should feel the stirring of an impulse, but instead of being in a great hurry to satisfy the urge just as quickly as possible, why not make up your mind to resist and attempt to sublimate it? Yes, catch hold of the energy as it begins to stir and direct it Heavenwards, all the way to the Divine Mother, to the

Heavenly Father. If young people would only practise this for a long time they could give a different orientation to their sexual energies and they would begin to sense what a truly spiritual love can be.

Remember what I told you about sacrifice: that it is very dangerous to give up an object, a habit or a desire without putting something else in its place. This is why you must never repress love, you must simply replace the thing you love with something new, something nobler and more luminous.

Let me give you an example: a man falls in love with a woman and feels that he cannot live without her. But she is not free; or perhaps it is he who is not free, he already has a wife; so they cannot live together without causing terrible problems to their two families. How can he conquer his longing for this woman? With the help of all women: instead of limiting himself to one woman, he must learn to love in his heart and soul all the women in the world. If he does this he will be so busy that he won't have time to chase after one of them and that is how all the women of the world will save him! And, of course, the method is equally valid for a woman. You must learn to broaden the scope of your consciousness otherwise you will be forever torn apart and in conflict with yourself. And suppose you have lost the one

you loved — either because he abandoned you or
because he is dead — you must replace him, but
not with another human being, for if you do that
you will simply run the risk of losing the second
one too: you must replace him by a great love for
a celestial, divine reality. If you do this, then you
will recapture inner peace and harmony, because
the void within you will have been filled.

Naturally, although it is to be hoped that
everyone make an effort in this area, it has not
been given to all men to attain perfect mastery of
their sexual energies in order to experience a
higher form of love. Before launching into such
an enterprise, therefore, it is important to think
about it very lucidly and, above all, to know oneself thoroughly. If you feel that you still need the
physical pleasures too much, then you would do
better not to deprive yourself of them all at once,
otherwise you will be worse off than before. But if
you are already highly evolved, and if you feel the
need to experience a subtler, more spiritual way of
life and to see and understand the marvels of the
divine world and help other human beings with
your love, then you are ready to choose this path.
But, I repeat: it is not for everyone. I certainly
don't advise it for those who are not ready,
because I know how many aberrations are possible in this area. Suppose that one marriage part-
ner decided he or she wanted to live a more

spiritual form of love whereas the other could not do without the physical pleasure: the situation could well become tragic. And in that case, of course, I know whose fault it would be: mine! I realize that I am running a risk in talking to you as I do about this, but I have to do it because I have to help those who are ready and anxious to evolve. But I know very well that there is a danger that I may be misunderstood and arouse hostility in some.

All I ask is that those who are listening to me today recognize the good sense in what I am saying and, above all, that they recognize that I have not the slightest desire to upset anybody's family but only to help men and women to broaden the scope of their awareness. If the ordinary, traditional conception of love produced good results there would be no need to change. But you can see for yourselves the kind of thing that goes on: domestic tragedies, suicides, murders and divorce! And even when a couple is together physically, they are often apart, the man thinking of the mistress he has — or dreams of having — and the woman of her lover! Even when they are outwardly faithful, in their hearts they are often cheating each other.

So this is why, even if you do not feel ready to live the higher degrees of love, you must still try to improve the way you love. Let me illustrate this: I have here two bottles of water. Now, let's say that one of them represents the wife and the other the husband. As both of them continually drink from the other, both bottles will soon be empty and it only remains to throw them away and get others. That is what happens if one has the ordinary conception of love : one drinks from a bottle whose capacity is, of course, limited and when it is empty one throws it away. Both bottles — both partners in a marriage — must be connected to the inexhaustible Fountainhead of love and in that way they will always be full, no one can ever drain their bottle dry because it will be permanently supplied with fresh water from the Source.

This means that if, instead of considering only the superficial aspects of the man or woman you love, you love their soul and spirit, then you will be linked to a live being, one that is already connected to the Source, to the Lord. In this way your love will last for ever : even when you are old and wrinkled you will still love each other because it is not the flesh you love but a living being, a reflection of the Godhead. Through his wife a man seeks the visage of the Divine Mother ; he raises himself towards Her so as to receive energy, light and love from Her. And a woman seeks to reach the Heavenly Father through her husband ; in this way their love will never come to an end. But if men and women are content to come together only on the lower levels they need not be surprised if they are soon disappointed. That is only to be expected: how can love be lasting if there is nothing good or beautiful to love beyond the physical body?

You can see how these things are reflected in the whole of nature: all that is opaque, dirty and impure tends to sink to the bottom, whereas that which is pure floats. And this holds true in human beings as well: in man, too, all that is coarse and cumbersome accumulates down below whereas all that is light, pure, luminous and subtle rises to the head. That is why the eyes, ears, mouth, nose and brain are all placed on the upper level, in the head, whereas other functions are placed lower down. The physical division of man, the upper and lower parts of his body, correspond to his higher and lower natures, the individuality and the personality. The personality is only interested in grabbing things for itself, in satisfying its appetites, so when love is manifested by the personality it is necessarily marred by these dense, obscure elements. Whereas love manifested by the individuality is marked by generosity and disinterestedness; it is pure and luminous.

When human beings love with a selfish, sensual love, they pass on to each other all kinds of dark, obscure elements which cloud their inner vision and prevent them from enjoying heavenly sensations. Obviously, they are free to do as they please; nobody is going to stop them from following their baser tendencies if they want to, but it is not in their best interests. If Initiates have given us certain rules and recommendations it is certainly not with the intention of taking all the joy out of love! On the contrary, it is in order to help human beings not to slip too far down into the lower levels of consciousness where they would be deprived of all the blessings and joys of the divine world.

From now on, therefore, make an effort to understand this sublime philosophy, for it is the only one which teaches men and women how to use the stimulus they give each other and the awe and delight they experience in the contemplation of each other; how to be continually inspired by these elements and use them to become geniuses and divinities.

But all this will only begin to be clear to your minds when you yourselves have made it clear through meditation and many inner adjustments. When you reach that point you will be in possession of all the treasures nature has prepared for you and capable of using them with the mathematical precision you would use in a laboratory. Then you will be capable of handling all these elements and forces and using them for your own regeneration and illumination and that of the whole world.

Editor-Distributor

Editions PROSVETA S.A. – B.P. 12 – 83601 Fréjus Cedex (France)

Distributors

AUSTRIA
MANDALA
Verlagauslieferung für Esoterik
A-6094 Axams, Innsbruckstraße 7

BELGIUM
PROSVETA BENELUX
Van Putlei 105 B-2548 Lint

N.V. MAKLU Somersstraat 13-15
B-2000 Antwerpen

VANDER S.A.
Av. des Volontaires 321
B-1150 Bruxelles

BRITISH ISLES
PROSVETA Ldt
The Doves Nest
Duddleswell Uckfield,
East Sussex TN 22 3JJ

Trade orders to :
ELEMENT Books Ltd
Unit 25 Longmead Shaftesbury
Dorset SP7 8PL

CANADA
PROSVETA Inc.
1565 Montée Masson
Duvernay est, Laval, Que. H7E 4P2

GERMANY
URANIA – Rudolf-Diesel-Ring 26
D-8029 Sauerlach

HOLLAND
STICHTING
PROSVETA NEDERLAND
Zeestraat 50
2042 LC Zandvoort

HONG KONG
HELIOS
31 New Kap Bin Long Village
Sai Kung N.T., Hong Kong

IRELAND
PROSVETA IRL.
84 Irishtown – Clonmel

ITALY
PROSVETA Coop. a.r.l.
Cas. post. 13046 – 20130 Milano

LUXEMBOURG
PROSVETA BENELUX
Van Putlei 105 B-2548 Lint

NORWAY
PROSVETA NORGE
Postboks 5101
1501 Moss

PORTUGAL
PUBLICAÇÕES
EUROPA-AMERICA Ltd
Est Lisboa-Sintra KM 14
2726 Mem Martins Codex

SPAIN
ASOCIACIÓN PROSVETA
Caspe 41
E-08010 Barcelona

SWITZERLAND
PROSVETA
Société Coopérative
CH - 1808 Les Monts-de-Corsier

UNITED STATES
PROSVETA U.S.A.
P.O. Box 49614
Los Angeles, California 90049

Dépôt légal : February 1988 – N° d'impression : 1583
Imprimerie PROSVETA, Z.I. du Capitou
B.P. 12 – 83601 Fréjus Cedex (France)
Imprimé en France